Seeds of Destruction

BOOKS BY THOMAS MERTON

The Asian Journal
Bread in the Wilderness
Conjectures of a Guilty Bystander
Contemplation in a World of Action
Disputed Questions
Gandhi on Non-Violence
Ishi Means Man
Life and Holiness
The Living Bread
Love and Living
The Monastic Journey
My Argument with the Gestapo
Mystics and Zen Masters
The New Man
New Seeds of Contemplation
No Man Is an Island
The Nonviolent Alternative
Seasons of Celebration
The Secular Journal of Thomas Merton
Seeds of Destruction
The Seven Storey Mountain
The Sign of Jonas
The Silent Life
Thoughts in Solitude
The Waters of Siloe
Zen and the Birds of Appetite

POETRY

The Collected Poems of Thomas Merton
Emblems of a Season of Fury
The Strange Islands
Selected Poems
The Tears of the Blind Lions

TRANSLATIONS

Clement of Alexandria
The Way of Chuang Tzu
The Wisdom of the Desert

of *Seeds* *Destruction*

By THOMAS MERTON

NEW YORK | *Farrar, Straus and Giroux*

Acknowledgment is made to the editors of Common-
weal, Jubilee, Ramparts, and Blackfriars in whose pages
these articles first appeared in somewhat different form.

Library of Congress Catalog Card Number 64-19515

What if God, desiring to show His wrath
And to make known His power,
Has endured with much patience
The vessels of wrath
Made for destruction?

Romans 9:22

Contents

AUTHOR'S NOTE

The contemplative life is not, and cannot be, a mere withdrawal, a pure negation, a turning of one's back on the world with its sufferings, its crises, its confusions and its errors. First of all, the attempt itself would be illusory. No man can withdraw completely from the society of his fellow men; and the monastic community is deeply implicated, for better or for worse, in the economic, political, and social structures of the contemporary world. To forget or to ignore this does not absolve the monk from responsibility for participation in events in which his very silence and "not knowing" may constitute a form of complicity. The mere fact of "ignoring" what goes on can become a political decision. Too often it has happened that contemplative communities in Europe, whose individual members were absorbed in other-worldly recollection, have officially and publicly given support to totalitarian movements. In such cases it can ultimately be said that the monk in his liturgy, in his study or in his contemplation is actually participating in those things he congratulates himself on having renounced.

This is not to say that the monk is obliged to partisan commitment, and that a contemplative should take this or that specific political line. On the contrary, the monk should be free of the confusions and falsities of partisan dispute. The last thing in the world I would want is a clerical or monastic movement in politics!

Yet I hold that the contemplative life of the Christian is not a life of abstraction, of secession, in order to concentrate upon ideal essences, upon absolutes, upon eternity alone. Christianity cannot reject history. It cannot be a denial of time. Christianity is centered on an historical event which has changed the meaning of history. The freedom of the Christian contemplative is not freedom *from* time, but freedom *in* time. It is the freedom to go out and meet God in the inscrutable mystery of His will here and now, in this precise moment in which He asks man's cooperation in shaping the course of history according to the demands of divine truth, mercy and fidelity.

The monastic flight from the world into the desert is not a mere refusal to know anything about the world, but a total rejection of all standards of judgment which imply attachment to a history of delusion, egoism and sin. Not of course a vain denial that the monk too is a sinner (this would be an even worse delusion), but a definitive refusal to participate in those activities which have no other fruit than to prolong the reign of untruth, greed, cruelty and arrogance in the world of men.

The monastic withdrawal from secular time is then not a retreat into an abstract eternity but a leap from the cyclic recurrence of inexorable evil into the eschatalogical Kingdom of God, in Christ —the kingdom of humility and of forgiveness.

The adversary is not time, not history, but the evil will and the accumulated inheritance of past untruth and past sin. This evil the monk must see. He must even denounce it, if others fail to do so.

What is the meaning of this "denunciation"? Is it to be regarded as a political act in the sense of an expressed determination to influence politics? Perhaps indirectly so. I speak not only as a monk but also as a responsible citizen of a very powerful nation. However, it is not my intention to imply that a state which is, and should be, secular, has to be guided by the perspectives of an eschatalogical Church. But I do intend to say at what point I and Christians who think as I do become morally obligated to dissent.

Therefore it seems to me to be a solemn obligation of conscience at this moment of history to take the positions which are indicated in the following pages. These positions are, it seems to me, in vital relation with the obligations I assumed when I took my monastic vows. To have a vow of poverty seems to me illusory if I do not in some way identify myself with the cause of people who are denied their rights and forced, for the most part, to live in abject misery. To have a vow of obedience seems to me to be absurd if it does not imply a deep concern for the most fundamental of all expressions of God's will: the love of His truth and of our neighbor.

Abbey of Gethsemani
July, 1964.

PART ONE

Black Revolution

LETTERS TO A WHITE LIBERAL

Introductory Note

These "Letters to a White Liberal" were written during the early summer of 1963 and revised in the fall of the same year. As they approach publication in book form, a few remarks are needed to situate them in the context in which they will quite probably be read.

The developments that have taken place during 1964 have, if anything, substantiated everything these "Letters" attempted to say.

The Civil Rights bill has been passed, after the longest debate in the history of Congress, after the longest filibuster, after the most sustained and energetic efforts to prevent its becoming law. The new legislation is, in the main, worthy of praise. But, as the "Letters" point out, it is one thing to have a law on the books and another to get the law enforced when in practice not only the

3

citizenry and "Citizens' Councils" but the police, the state governments and the courts themselves are often in league against the Federal government. To what extent the law will remain a dead letter in the South, to what extent it will simply aggravate pressures and animosities in the North, where such righs are still guaranteed in theory more than in practice, is not quite possible to predict.

One thing is certain: since this law will not be entirely enforced, and since, even if it were perfectly enforced it would still not be able to meet critical problems that are more strictly economic and sociological (jobs, housing, delinquency, irresponsible violence), we are forced to admit that the Civil Rights legislation is not the end of the battle but only *the beginning of a new and more critical phase in the conflict.*

How comforting, how utopian a thought, if we could only convince ourselves that this new law marks the final victory in a patient and courageous struggle of moderate leaders, dedicated to non-violence and to scrupulous respect for social order and ethical principles! It is true of course that Birmingham and the Washington March in 1963 were symbolic of a long non-violent fight for rights. They marked the final stages of the campaign that made the Civil Rights bill an urgent necessity.

At the same time the systematic lawlessness and violence with which the opponents of Civil Rights legislation have set their own "rights" above those guaranteed by the law, have effectively undermined the respect which the Negroes themselves may have had for the legal and administrative agencies that are supposed to keep order and protect rights. Thus the struggle for the bill has also demonstrated that, in order to exercise the rights which the law protects, the Negro (and anyone else whose rights are in fact denied) is going to have to obtain some form of power.

Of course the law specifically removes obstacles to the registration and voting of Negroes, reaffirming that they should have access to the democratic exercise of power by ballot. Obviously, however, it is going to be a long time before Negroes can make full use of this particular form of power. And the use of molotov cocktails and bullets against them when they attempt to vote, unfortunately encourages them to prefer bullets to ballots themselves.

So it happens that now, after the passage of the bill, a new, tougher Negro leadership promises to emerge, no longer moderate and non-violent, and much more disposed to make sinister and effective use of the threat of force implied by the great concentration of frustrated, angry and workless Negroes in the ghettoes of the North. We can now expect violent, though perhaps disorganized and sporadic, initiatives in force around the edges of the Negro slums. This is already a familiar experience in some cities where, however, the violence has usually been designated under the rubric of "deliquency" rather than that of "revolution." But let us not forget that delinquency itself is simply a spontaneous form of non-political protest and revolt.

When the Civil Rights bill passed, a Southern Senator tragically declared that this would "only add to the hatred." He was of course right in foreseeing that after the bill became law the danger of hatred and violence would be even greater than before. But he was not necessarily right in attributing this to the law as such. He simply knew that the law had not ended the struggle. He knew well enough that the law had left the white South more deeply and grimly entrenched in its refusals. That the Negro, North and South, was more determined to take matters into his own hands, since he was convinced that even the liberal white man was not prepared to give him anything beyond fair promises and a certain abstract good will.

No one can be blind to the possibilities of violence in this situation. Though it is quite true that the vast majority both of whites and Negroes want to solve this problem without force and bloodshed, their "wanting" and their good intentions are no longer enough. It is also obvious that the majority of Americans were shocked and appalled by the senseless murder of President Kennedy. The fact remains that no matter who may have been guilty of actually shooting the President the murder grew out of the soil of hatred and violence that then existed and still exists in the South. It has been said often enough, but not too often, that the President had already been killed a thousand times over by the thoughts and the words, spoken or printed, of the racists. His death was something that had been meditated, imagined, desired and "needed" in a profound and savage way that made it in some sense inevitable. This was something that John F. Kennedy himself evidently did not understand, or he would have gone into Dallas that day with less confidence and better protection. It is also something that the majority of Americans still do not quite manage to believe. But it must be affirmed: *where minds are full of hatred and where imaginations dwell on cruelty, torment, punishment, revenge and death, then inevitably there will be violence and death.*

Why, in this particular crisis (and this applies to international politics as well as to domestic or economic upheaval), is there so much hatred and so dreadful a need for explosive violence? Because of the impotency and the frustration of a society that sees itself involved in difficulties which, though this may not consciously be admitted, promise to be insuperable. Actually, there is no reason why they *should* be insuperable, but as long as white society persists in clinging to its present condition and to its own image of itself as the only acceptable reality, then the problem will remain without reasonable solution, and there will inevitably be violence.

The problem is this: if the Negro, as he actually is (not the "ideal" and theoretical Negro, or even the educated and cultured Negro of the small minority), enters wholly into white society, then *that society is going to be radically changed.* This of course is what the white South very well knows, and it is what the white Liberal has failed to understand. Not only will there be a radical change which, whatever form it may take, will amount to at least a peaceful revolution, but also there will be enormous difficulties and sacrifices demanded of everyone, especially the whites. Obviously property values will be affected. The tempo of life and its tone will be altered. The face of business and professional life may change. The approach to the coming crucial labor and economic problems will be even more anguished than we have feared. The psychological adjustment alone will be terribly demanding, perhaps even more for Negroes than for whites in many cases.

These are things which the South is able to see. But their reality does not justify the conservative conclusion which clings blindly to the present impossible state of things, and determines to preserve it at any cost, even that of a new civil war. We must dare to pay the dolorous price of change, *to grow into a new society*. Nothing else will suffice!

The only way out of this fantastic impasse is for everyone to face and accept the difficulties and sacrifices involved, in all their seriousness, in all their inexorable demands. This is what our society, based on a philosophy of every man for himself and on the rejection of altruism and sacrifice (except in their most schematic and imaginary forms) is not able to do. Yet it is something which it must learn to do. It cannot begin to learn unless it knows the need to learn. These "Letters" attempt to demonstrate the reality of that need and the urgency of the situation.

I.   If I dare to imagine that these letters may have some significance for both of us, it is because I believe that Christianity is concerned with human crises, since Christians are called to manifest the mercy and truth of God in history.

Christianity is the victory of Christ in the world—that is to say, in history. It is the salvation of man in and through history, through temporal decisions made for love of Christ, the Redeemer and Lord of History. The mystery of Christ is at work in all human events, and our comprehension of secular events works itself out and expresses itself in that sacred history, the history of salvation, which the Holy Spirit teaches us to perceive in events that appear to be purely secular. We have to admit that this meaning is often provisional and sometimes beyond our grasp. Yet as Christians we are committed to an attempt to read an ultimate and transcendent meaning in temporal events that flow from human choices. To be specific, we are bound to search "history," that is to say the intelligible actions of men, for some indications of their inner significance, and *some relevance to our commitment as Christians.*

"History" then is for us that complex of mean-

ings which we read into the interplay of acts and
decisions that make up our civilization. And we
are also (this is more urgent still) at a turning
point in the history of that European and American society which has been shaped and dominated
by Christian concepts, even where it has at times
been unfaithful to its basically Christian vocation.
We live in a culture which seems to have reached
the point of extreme hazard at which it may
plunge to its own ruin, unless there is some renewal of life, some new direction, some providential reorganization of its forces for survival.

Pope Paul VI, in opening the second session of
Vatican Council II, has clearly spelled out the
obligation of the Church to take the lead in this
renewal by becoming aware of her own true
identity and her vocation in the world of today.
He has said without any hesitation or ambiguity
that the Church must recognize her duty to manifest Christ to the world, and must therefore strive
as far as possible to resemble the hidden Lord of
Ages so as to make Him visible in her charity,
her love of truth and her love of man. To that end,
the Church has the obligation to purify and renew
her inner life, because it is "only after this work of
internal sanctification has been accomplished that
the Church will be able to show herself to
the whole world and say: 'Who sees me sees

Christ.' "* In order to do this the Church herself must "look upon Christ to discern her true
likeness."

Now this call to a universal examination of
conscience, not only on the part of Catholics but
also implicitly of all Christians, came exactly two
weeks after a bomb exploded in a Baptist Church
in Birmingham, Alabama, killing four Negro
girls at Sunday School. On that same day, in the
same city, an Eagle scout, of the white race who
had been to Sunday School *and* to a racist rally,
shot and killed a twelve year old Negro boy for
no other reason than that he was a Negro.

These were not the actions of Catholics, but
they took place in a region where many Catholics
have explicitly and formally identified themselves
with racial segregation and therefore with the
denial of certain vital civil rights to Negroes. In
Louisiana, not long before the Pope's address,
Catholics had set fire to a parochial school rather
than allow it to be opened to Negro students
along with white. In Louisiana also a Catholic
priest who had white and Negro children receive
their first communion at the same time, though at
different ends of the altar rail, was beaten up by
his parishioners for this affront to Southern dignity.
(In most Catholic Churches of the South, Negro
communicants may only approach the altar rail

* Opening address of Pope Paul, September 29, 1963.

after all the whites have departed.) In the light of these events, the following words of Pope Paul have a special seriousness and urgency: "If (the Church) were to discover some shadow, some defect, some stain upon her wedding garment, what should be her instinctive, courageous reaction? There can be no doubt that her primary duty would be to reform, correct, and set herself aright in conformity with her divine Model."

At present, in a worldwide struggle for power which is entirely pragmatic, if not cynically un-principled, the claims of those who appeal to their Christian antecedents as justification for their struggle to maintain themselves in power are being judged by the events which flow from their supposedly "Christian" choices.

For example, we belong to a nation which prides itself on being free, and which relates this freedom at least implicitly to its source in Chris-tian theology. Our freedom rests on respect for the rights of the human person, and though our society is not officially Christian, this democratic respect for the person can be traced to the Chris-tian concept that every man is to be regarded as Christ, and treated as Christ.

Briefly, then: we justify our policies, whether national or international, by the implicit postulate that we are supremely concerned with the human person and his rights. We do this because our ancestors regarded every man as Christ, wished to treat him as Christ, or at least believed this to be the right way to act, even though they did not always follow this belief.

Now if we advance this claim, and base our decisions and choices upon it, we must not be surprised if the claim itself comes under judgment. If we assert that we are the guardians of peace, freedom, and the rights of the person, we may expect other people to question this, demanding, from time to time, some evidence that we mean what we say. Commonly they will look for that evidence in our actions. And if our actions do not fit our words, they will assume that we are either fools, deceiving ourselves, or liars attempting to deceive others.

Our claims to high-minded love of freedom and our supposed defense of Christian and personalist ideals are going to be judged, we believe, not only by other men, but above all by God. At times we are perhaps rashly inclined to find this distinction reassuring. We say to ourselves: God at least knows our sincerity. He does not suspect us as our enemies do. He sees the *reality* of our good intentions!

I am sure He sees whatever reality is there. But are we absolutely certain that He judges our intentions exactly as we do?

Let me cite an example. Our defense policies

and the gigantic arms race which they require are all based on the supposition that we seek peace and freedom, not only for ourselves, but for the whole world. We claim to possess the only effective and basically sincere formula for world peace because we alone are truly honest in our claim to respect the human person. For us, the person and his freedom with his basic rights to life, liberty and the pursuit of happiness, comes absolutely first. Therefore the sincerity and truth of all our asserted aims, at home and abroad, in defense and in civil affairs, is going to be judged by the *reality* of our respect for persons and for their rights. The rest of the world knows this very well. We seem not to have realized this as well as they.

We fail to notice that the plans we have devised for defending the human person and his freedom involve the destruction of millions of human persons in a few minutes, not because the great majority of these persons are themselves hostile to us, or a threat to us, but because by destroying them we hope to destroy a *system* which is hostile to us and which in addition, is tyrannizing over them, reducing them to abject servitude, and generally destroying their rights and dignities as human persons. Their oppressors have taken away their rights—but we will compound the injury by also taking away their lives and this in the name of the "person" and of "freedom"!

At the same time, even those who believe that such a war could conceivably be "won," admit that we ourselves, the prospective victors, would necessarily have to live for many years under a military dictatorship while undergoing reconstruction.

Clearly, a defense policy that leads to the outright destruction of millions of innocent persons and to the severe curtailing of liberties, even of those who have fought for liberty and won, may be accounted a valid defense of a *system,* or an organization, but it is in no sense a defense of persons and personal rights, since it sacrifices these to the supposed interests of the system. In that case, it is not really the person and his rights who come first, but the system. Not flesh and blood, but an abstraction.

Another example: we claim that we are really solicitous for the rights of the Negro, and willing to grant him these rights some time or other. We even insist that the very nature of our society is such that the Negro, as a person, is precisely what we respect the most. Our laws declare that we are not simply a society which tolerates the presence of the Negro as a second class citizen of whom we would prefer to rid ourselves altogether if we only could. They assert that since the Negro is a person, he is in every way equal to every other person, and must enjoy the same rights as every other person. Our religion adds that what we do to him, we do to Christ, since we are a free society, based on respect for the dignity of the human person as taught to the world by Christianity.

How, then, do we treat this other Christ, this person, who happens to be black?

First, if we look to the south which is plentifully supplied not only with Negroes but also with professed Christian believers, we discover that belief in the Negro as a person is accepted only with serious qualifications, while the notion that he is to be treated as Christ has been overlooked. It would not be easy for a Christian to mutilate another man, string him up on a tree and shoot him full of holes if he believed that what he did to that man was done to Christ. On the contrary, he must somehow imagine that he is doing this to the devil—to prevent the devil doing it to him. But in thinking such thoughts, a Christian has spiritually apostatized from Christianity and has implicitly rejected that basic respect for the rights of the person on which a truly Christian and free society depends. From then on anything such a man may say about "Christianity" or "freedom" has lost all claim to rational significance.

Only with the greatest unwillingness have some very earnest Southern Christians, under duress, accepted the painful need to ride in the same part of public conveyances with Negroes, eat at the same lunch counters, use the same public facilities. And there are still not a few of these Christians who absolutely refuse to worship Christ in the same congregations as Negroes. Even some Catholics have refused to receive the Body of Christ together with Negroes in sacramental communion: and they have been astonished to find themselves excommunicated officially for refusing integrated schools, when in point of fact they had already by their own action manifestly excommunicated themselves, acting implicitly as schismatics, rending the unity of the Body of Christ.

Nevertheless, the inner conflicts and contradictions of the South are not to be taken as a justification for the smugness with which the North is doing just as poor a job, if not a worse job, of defending the Negro's rights as a person. The race "problem" is something which the southerner cannot escape. Almost half the population of the South are Negroes. Though there are greater concentrations of Negroes in northern slums, yet northern Negroes can be treated as if they were not there at all. For years, New Yorkers have been able to drive to Westchester and Connecticut without going through Harlem, or even seeing it, except from a distant freeway. The abuses thus tolerated and ignored are sometimes as bad and worse than anything in the South.

It is clear that our actual decisions and choices,

with regard to the Negro, show us that in fact we are not interested in the rights of several million persons, who are members and citizens of our society and are in every way loyal Americans. They pay taxes, fight for the country and do as well as anybody else in meeting their responsibilities. And yet we tolerate shameful injustices which deprive them, by threats and by actual violence, of their right to vote and to participate actively in the affairs of the nation.

Here I can see you will protest. You will point to the Supreme Court decisions that have upheld Negro rights, to education in integrated colleges and schools. It seems to me that our motives are judged by the real fruit of our decisions. What have we done? We have been willing to grant the Negro rights on paper, even in the South. But the laws have been framed in such a way that in every case their execution has depended on the good will of white society, and the white man has not failed, when left to himself, to block, obstruct, or simply forget the necessary action without which the rights of the Negro cannot be enjoyed in fact. Hence, when laws have been passed, then contested, dragged through all the courts, and finally upheld, the Negro is still in no position to benefit by them without, in each case, entering into further interminable lawsuits every time he

wants to exercise a right that is guaranteed to him
by law.

In effect, we are not really giving the Negro a
right to live where he likes, eat where he likes,
go to school where he likes or work where he likes,
but only *to sue the white man who refuses to let
him do these things*. If every time I want an ice
cream soda I have to sue the owner of the drug-
store, I think I will probably keep going to the
same old places in my ghetto. That is what the
Negro, until recently, has done. Such laws are
without meaning unless they reflect a willingness
on the part of white society to implement them.

You will say: "You cannot legislate morality."
That phrase may be quite true in its own proper
context. But here it is a question not of "morality"
but of social order. If we have got to the point
where the laws are frequently, if not commonly,
framed in such a way that they can be easily
evaded by a privileged group, then the very structure of our society comes into question. If you are
knowingly responsible for laws that will be systematically violated, then you are partly to blame
for the disorders and the confusion resulting from
civil disobedience and even revolution.

I think there is possibly some truth in the
accusation that we are making laws simply because
they look nice on the books. Having them there,
we can enjoy the comfort of pointing to them,

reassuring our own consciences, convincing ourselves that we are all that we claim to be, and
refuting the vicious allegations of critics who
question the sincerity of our devotion to freedom.

But at the same time, when our own personal
interests and preferences are concerned, we have
no intention of respecting the Negro's rights in
the concrete; North or South, integration is always going to be not on our street but "somewhere else." That perhaps accounts for the extraordinary zeal with which the North insists
upon integration in the South, while treating the
Northern Negro as if he were invisible, and flatly
refusing to let him take shape in full view, lest he
demand the treatment due to a human person and
a free citizen of this nation.

That is why the Negro now insists on making
himself just as obviously visible as he can. That is
why he demonstrates. He has come to realize that
the white man is less interested in the rights of
the Negro than in the white man's own spiritual
and material comfort. If then, by making himself visible, the Negro can finally disturb the
white man's precious "peace of soul," then by all
means he would be a fool not to do so.

Yet when we are pressed and criticized, and
when the Negro's violated rights are brought up
before us, we stir ourselves to renewed efforts at
legislation, we introduce more bills into Congress,

knowing well enough how much chance those bills have of retaining any real significance after they have finally made it (if they make it at all).

The Negro finally gets tired of this treatment and becomes quite rightly convinced that the only way he is ever going to get his rights is by fighting for them himself. But we deplore his demonstrations, we urge him to go slow, we warn him against the consequences of violence (when, at least so far, most of the organized violence has been on our side and not on his). At the same time we secretly desire violence, and even in some cases *provoke* it, in the hope that the whole Negro movement for freedom can be repressed by force.

I do not claim to be a prophet or even a historian. I do not profess to understand all the mysteries of political philosophy, but I question whether our claims to be the only sincere defenders of the human person, of his rights, of his dignity, of his nobility as a creature made in God's image, as a member of the Mystical Body of Christ, can be substantiated by our actions. It seems to me that we have retained little more than a few slogans and concepts that have been emptied of reality.

It seems to me that we have little genuine interest in human liberty and in the human person. What we are interested in, on the contrary, is the unlimited freedom of the corporation. When we call ourselves the "free world" we mean first of all the world in which *business* is free. And the freedom of the person comes only after that, because, in our eyes, the freedom of the person is dependent on money. That is to say, without money, freedom has no meaning. And therefore the most basic freedom of all is the freedom to make money. If you have nothing to buy or sell, freedom is, in your case, irrelevant. In other words, what we are really interested in is not *persons*, but *profits*. Our society is organized first and foremost with a view to business, and wherever we run into a choice between the rights of a human person and the advantage of a profit-making organization, the rights of the person will have difficulty getting a hearing. Profit first, people afterward.

You ask me, indignantly, to confirm these vicious allegations?

It appears that the one aspect of the Negro demonstrations that is being taken most seriously in the South is that *they hurt business.* As long as there was talk only of "rights," and of "freedom" (concepts which imply *persons*) the Negro movement was taken seriously chiefly by crackpots, idealists, and members of suspicious organizations thought to be under direct control of Moscow, like CORE and the NAACP.

All this talk of Negro rights, especially when

accompanied by hymn-singing and religious exhortations, could hardly be taken seriously!

*It was only when money became involved that
the Negro demonstrations finally impressed themselves upon the American mind as being real.*

We claim to judge reality by the touchstone of
Christian values, such as freedom, reason, the
spirit, faith, personalism, etc. In actual fact we
judge them by commercial values: sales, money,
price, profits. It is not the life of the spirit that is
real to us, but the vitality of the *market*. Spiritual
values are to us, in actual fact, meaningless unless
they can be reduced to terms of buying and selling. But buying and selling are abstract operations.
Money has no ontological reality: it is a pure convention. Admittedly it is a very practical one. But
it is in itself completely unreal, and the ritual that
surrounds money transactions, the whole liturgy
of marketing and of profit, is basically void of
reality and of meaning. Yet we treat it as the final
reality, the absolute meaning, in the light of
which everything else is to be judged, weighed,
evaluated, and "priced."

Thus we end up by treating persons as objects
for sale, and therefore as meaningless unless they
have some value on the market. A man is to us
nothing more nor less than "what he is worth."
He is "known" to us as a reality when he is known

to be solvent by bankers. Otherwise he has not yet begun to exist.

Our trouble is that we are alienated from our own personal reality, our true self. We do not believe in anything but money and the power or the enjoyment which come from the possession of money. We do not believe in ourselves, except in so far as we can estimate our own worth, and verify, by our operations in the world of the market, that our subjective price coincides with what society is willing to pay for us.

And the Negro? He has so far been worth little or nothing.

Until quite recently there was no place for him in our calculations, unless perhaps we were landlords—unless we had *real* estate—in Harlem. That of course was another matter, because the Negro was, after all, quite profitable to us. And yet we did not think of profit as coming to us from the beings of flesh and blood, human persons, who were crowded into those rooms. On the contrary, it came to us from the only thing that was *real*—our estate. The Negro was so shadowy, so unreal, that he was nothing more than the occasion for a series of very profitable transactions which gave us a good solid reality in our own eyes and in the eyes of our society.

But now, suddenly, we have discovered that there are also some "real" Negroes. For them to be real, they must have the same kind of reality as ourselves. Reality is estimated in terms of (financial) worth. And so we are delighted to discover that there are a few Negroes who have money.

Why has this rich Negro suddenly earned our benevolent attention? Because he is a person, because he has brains, because of the fantastic talents which alone could enable him to be a professional success against such inhuman odds? None of this. It is now to our interest to recognize him, because we can use him against the others. So now, when the Negro claims he wants to take his full part in American society as a *person*, we retort: you already are playing your part as a person: "Negroes over the years," we now declare, "have had a rapid rise in income." (A nice vague statement, but it satisfies the mind of anyone who believes in money.) "Large numbers of Negroes drive high-priced cars." Another beautiful act of faith! But here we come with "exact figures":

"It is estimated that there are now thirty-five Negro millionaires in the United States."

What are these statements supposed to mean? Simply that there is no need for the Negro to make such a fuss, to demonstrate, to fight for recognition as a person. He has *received that recognition already*. "Thirty-five Negroes are millionaires." (Thirty-five out of twenty million!) "Large numbers" drive "high-priced cars." What more do you want? These are indications that the Negro has all he needs, for he has "opportunities," he can make money and thus become real.

What opportunities?

Even though a Negro millionaire may live in a "fine residential neighborhood" he is still living in a ghetto, because when he moves in, the whites move out. The neighborhood is taken over by Negroes, and even if they are millionaires, their presence means that a neighborhood is no longer "fine." For a white man it is no longer even "residential."

So that even when he is worth a million, a Negro cannot buy himself, in the land of the free, the respect that is given to a human person.

Doubtless the mercy and truth of God, the victory of Christ, are being manifested in our current history, but I am not able to see how they are being manifested *by us*.

II.   A little time, perhaps only a
few more months, and we will realize that we
have reached a moment of unparalleled seriousness
in American history, indeed in the history of the
world. The word "revolution" is getting around.
Accepted at first with tolerance, as a pleasantly
vivid figure of speech, it is going to be regarded
with more and more disapproval, because it comes
too near to the truth. And why? What is a revolution? What does it mean to say that the Negro's
struggle for full civil rights amounts to a revolution?

Much as it might distress southerners, the fact
that a Negro may now sit down next to a white
woman at a snack bar and order a sandwich is
still somewhat short of revolution. And if by dint
of courageous and effective protest the Negroes
who have a vote in deep southern states should
actually manage to cast their votes on election day
without getting shot: that in itself does not make
a revolution, though it may have something radically new about it. The question is, who will they
be voting for? Ross Barnett?

Yet I have often thought there is something
true, as well as sinister, in the usual conservative

claim to "realism." We must admit that the
southern politicians are much more fully aware of
the revolutionary nature of the situation than are
those northern liberals who blithely suppose that
somehow the Negroes (both north and south)
will gradually and quietly "fit in" to white society exactly as it is, with its affluent economy,
the mass media, its political machines, and the
professional inanity of its middle class suburban
folkways.

We seem to think that when the Negroes of
the south really begin to *use* their largely hypo-
thetical right to vote, they will be content with
the same candidates who were up last year and the
year before. If those candidates themselves were
under any such illusion, they would have long
since done something that would get them the
Negro votes.

In point of fact, the southern politicians realize
very well that if the Negroes turn out full force to
vote, and thereby establish themselves as a factor
to be reckoned with in southern politics, the
political machines of the past are going to collapse
in a cloud of dust. To put it succinctly: if the
southern Negro is really granted the rights which
are guaranteed to him, *de jure,* by the American
Constitution, and if he fully and freely exercises
those rights, it is all up with the old South. There
are quite enough Negroes in the South to make

any really free election catastrophic for the *status quo*. And Negroes, both South and North, are not going to waste time voting for people who sick police dogs on them and drench them with high pressure firehoses, while occasionally lobbing a bomb onto their front porches for good measure.

So much for the South. But what about the North? Northern Negroes are perhaps able to put a candidate or two of their own into office: but this is only the beginning of what is suddenly becoming a very conscious and concerted drive for real political power.

In the fall of 1963, after the spectacular success of the Washington March (a success which the Negroes themselves regarded as highly ambiguous), steps were taken to form a new political party consisting mostly of Negroes. The "Freedom Now Party" is likely to have a considerable effect on American politics. While in the South we can doubt that Negroes will risk their lives to vote for Southern white politicians, there is every likelihood that they will become more active if they see a chance of getting candidates of their own. And the mere fact of their *attempting* such a thing is likely to throw the South into revolutionary turmoil. In the North, on the other hand, the big cities are now largely populated by Negroes (the whites live in the suburbs) and the

Negroes can perhaps without too much difficulty gain control of urban congressional districts.

This drive for political power is going to be more and more accelerated by the problem of jobs. With five million unemployed officially acknowledged in 1963, with no indications other than that this figure *must grow,* and with repeated strikes and protests in which Negroes demand to be hired along with whites, there is going to be violent conflict over the limited number of jobs. With the best will in the world, nobody is going to be able to give jobs to Negroes without taking them away from whites, and there is no indication, at the moment, that the whites intend to retire *en masse* and spend the rest of their lives watching TV so that the Negroes may carry on the work, and collect the paychecks, of the nation.

This represents, whether we like it or not, a radical threat to our present system—a revolutionary situation. And furthermore it accentuates the already clearly defined racial lines dividing the two sides in the conflict. This means that the Negro is going to continue to be what he has decidedly become: aggressively aware of the impact on white society of the mere *threat* of revolutionary violence.

The Negro finds himself in the presence of a social structure which he has reason to consider inherently unjust (since it has seldom done him

any real justice except in fair words and promises).
He also sees that this society has suddenly become
extremely vulnerable. The very agitation and confusion which greet his demands are to him indications of guilt and fear, and he has very little
respect for exhortations to "go slow" and "be
patient." He feels he has been patient for a very
long time and that anyone who cannot see this for
himself is not being honest about it. He also feels
that there is no hope of any action being taken
unless he takes action himself, and that the steps
taken by the government are mere political ma-
neuvers leading nowhere.

This means that a well-meaning liberal policy
of compromises and concessions, striving at the
same time to placate the Negro and to calm the
seething indignation of the conservative whites, is
not going to avert danger. It may, on the contrary
aggravate it. Hence the "realism" again, of the
conservatives, who think that the only thing is to
stop violence now by the full use of all the repressive agencies—police, national guard, army,
—which they themselves still fully control. After
all, the traditional line of thought of those who use
repressive power to defend the *status quo,* is that
they are justified in applying force to prevent a
chaotic and explosive outbreak of revolutionary
disorder, save many lives, protect property (especially their own, of course) and maintain a sem-

blance of national identity which would otherwise
be dissolved in blood. Needless to say, this is
identical with the argument which revolutionaries
themselves advance for repressing all resistance
once they themselves have achieved their aim and
have seized full power.

Now, my liberal friend, here is your situation.
You, the well-meaning liberal, are right in the
middle of all this confusion. You are, in fact, a
political catalyst. On the one hand, with your
good will and your ideals, your fine hopes and
your generous, but vague, love of mankind in the
abstract and of rights enthroned on a juridical
Olympus, you offer a certain encouragement to
the Negro (and you do right, my only complaint
being that you are not yet right enough) so that,
abetted by you, he is emboldened to demand concessions. Though he knows you will not support
all his demands, he is well aware that you will be
forced to support some of them in order to maintain your image of yourself as a liberal. He also
knows, however, that your material comforts, your
security, and your congenial relations with the
establishment are much more important to you
than your rather volatile idealism, and that when
the game gets rough you will be quick to see your
own interests menaced by his demands. And you
will sell him down the river for the five hundredth
time in order to protect yourself. For this reason,

as well as to support your own self-esteem, you are very anxious to have a position of leadership and control in the Negro's fight for rights, in order to be able to apply the brakes when you feel it is necessary.

This is probably one of the main reasons why you turned out for the Washington March. Doubtless you were not thinking of any such thing, and I am not questioning your sincerity or your generosity. But there are unconscious motives in political action as well as everywhere else. They must be taken into account. Whatever may have been your conscious motives at Washington, whatever may be the reality of your optimism about the results of the March (and let us admit that it was in many ways admirable), the Negro feels that your principal contribution was to make the whole issue ambiguous and remove its revolutionary sting. He feels that you once again obscured the real issue, which is that American society *has to change* before the race problem can be solved. The atmosphere of congenial fraternity and nobility which marked the great demonstration, and certainly made it edifying from many points of view, seemed once again to indicate that liberal optimism and fair weather principles would be enough, and that the Negro would move into the place that belongs to him in white American society. But to the Negro, that is only a liberal myth. He knows that there is at present *no place for him* whatever in American society, except at the bottom of the totem pole.

Any form of social protest that assumes that the Negro has a place ready and waiting for him, in American society, is simply irrelevant, a mystification, and a fraudulent deception. The Negro has now become very alert to detect such impostures. Indeed he has become obsessively intent upon the slightest indication of fraud, so much so that he overlooks other aspects of the situation, and does not observe, for instance, that though you thought you were in the Washington March because the Negro needed you there, you were really on the march because *you needed to be there*. The health of your soul demanded it, and for that reason I am glad that you were there, and wish that I had been there with you. But the private needs of your liberal conscience are of absolutely no interest to the Negro who has a much more urgent problem to solve. And your presence is not necessarily helping him to solve it.

This is why the Negro has mixed feelings about your support. He does not want you in his way. You are more of a nuisance than anything else. And you, offended at this lack of appreciation, want to reassure the Negro—you are really on his side, and to prove it you will help him to get just a little more. You will be satisfied with the headlines. You will once again feel cozy with your liberal image—for a few days. Thus you make it possible for him, according to the fantasies of conservative thought to "taste blood." And conservative thought is not always deluded in its choice of metaphors.

On the other hand, when you come face to face at last with *concrete* reality, and take note of some unexpected and unlovely aspects of what you have hitherto considered only in the abstract, you yourself are going to be a very frightened mortal. You are going to see that there are more than ideas and ideals involved in this struggle. It is more than a matter of images and headlines. And you are going to realize that what has begun is not going to be stopped, but that it will lead on into a future for which the past, perhaps, offers little or no precedent. But since it is one of the characteristics of liberals that they prefer their future to be vaguely predictable (just as the conservative prefers only a future that reproduces the past in all its details), when you see that the future is entirely out of your hands and that you are totally unprepared for it, you are going to fall back on the past, and you are going to end up in the arms of the conservatives. Indeed, you will be so much in their arms that you will be in their way, and will not improve the shooting.

These are frank and brutal facts, my good

friend. But they are the facts on which you must base your future decisions. You must face it: this upheaval is going to sweep away not only the old style political machines, the quaint relics of a more sanguine era, but also a great deal of the managerial sophistication of our own time. And your liberalism is likely to go out the window along with a number of other entities that have their existence chiefly on paper and in the head.

What are you going to do? Are you going to say that though changes may be desirable in theory, they cannot possibly be paid for by a social upheaval amounting to revolution? Are you going to decide that the Negro movement is already out of hand, and therefore it must be stopped at any cost, even at the cost of ruthless force? In that case, you are retreating from the unknown future and falling back on a known and familiar alternative: namely the alternative in which you, who are after all on top, *remain on top by the use of force,* rather than admit a change in which you will not necessarily be on the bottom, but in which your position as top dog will no longer be guaranteed. You will prefer your own security to everything else, and you will be willing to sacrifice the Negro to preserve yourself.

But it is precisely in this that you are contributing to the inexorable development of a revolution, for revolutions are always the result of situations in which the drive of an underprivileged mass of men can no longer be contained by token concessions, and in which the establishment is too confused, too inert and too frightened to *participate* with the underprivileged in a new and creative solution of what is realized to be *their common problem*.

Is this the case at present in the United States? Instead of seeing the Negro revolution as a manifestation of a deep disorder that is eating away the inner substance of our society, *because it is in ourselves,* do we look at it only as a threat from outside ourselves—as an unjust and deplorable infringement of our rights by an irresponsible minority, goaded on by Red agitators? This would be a totally fanciful view, which removes the crisis from the context of reality into a dreamworld of our own in which we proceed to seek a dream-solution. Have we forgotten that the Negro is there *because of us?* His crisis is the result of our acts, and is, in fact *our crisis.* Inability to see this might turn a common political problem into a violent conflict, in which there would be no possibility of real dialogue, and in which the insensate shibboleths of racism would drown out all hope of rational solutions. If this should happen, even those whites and Negroes who would normally be able to work together to find a common solution, will be driven apart, and the white man will become the black man's enemy by the mere fact that he is white.

As Martin Luther King sees so clearly, if the Negro struggle becomes a violent conflict (and this is what would best please the racists whether white or black!) it is bound to fail in its most rational and creative purpose—the real vindication of Negro rights and the definitive assertion of the Negro as a person equal in dignity to any other human person.

"I am convinced," says Dr. King, "that if we succumb to the temptation to use violence in our struggle for freedom, unborn generations will be the recipients of a long and desolate night of bitterness; our chief legacy to them will be a never-ending reign of chaos."*

In one word, there is a serious possibility of an eventual civil war which might wreck the fabric of American society. And although the Negro revolution in America is now unquestionably non-Marxist, and just as unquestionably a completely original and home-grown product of our own, there is no doubt that if it resulted in a violent upheaval of American economic and political life, there might be a danger of Marxist elements "capturing" the revolution and taking it over in the name of Soviet Communism. Remote as it may seem, this fits an already familiar pattern,

* From *Strength to Love*, Harper, 1963.

and furthermore it has to be considered because it already dominates the minds of the segregationist right wing.

My question to you is this: can you think of a better way of conducting yourself?

Does all profoundly significant social change have to be carried out in violence, with murder, destruction, police repression and underground resistance? Is it not possible that the whites might give closer attention to the claims of Negro leaders like Martin Luther King, who assert that they do not want violence, and who give every assurance (backed up by some rather convincing evidence, if you can remember Birmingham) that the Negro is not out to kill anybody, that he is really fighting not only for his own freedom, but also, in some strange way, for the freedom of the whites. (This is a new and quixotic concept to us, since we are fully convinced that we are the freest people that ever existed.)

Is it true that even the smallest change of our present social framework is necessarily a disaster so great that any price, however immoral, can legitimately be paid to keep it from coming about? Is it not possible that whites and Negroes might join together in a creative political experiment such as the world has never yet seen, and in which the first condition would be that the whites consented to let the Negroes run their own revolution non-violently, giving them the necessary support and cooperation, and not being alarmed at some of the sacrifices and difficulties that would necessarily be involved?

Is there no alternative but violent repression, in which, reluctantly no doubt, you decide that it is better for the establishment to be maintained by the exercise of the power which is entirely in white hands, and which ought to remain in white hands because they are white (because, of course, Negroes are "not ready" for any kind of power)?

This presupposes a simple view of the situation: a belief that when the chips are down it is going to be either whites or blacks and since whites have proved their capacity to "run the country" and "keep order," it is unthinkable even to permit the possibility of that disorder which, you take it for granted, would follow if Negroes took a leading part in our political life.

Conclusion: revolution must be prevented at all costs; but demonstrations are already revolutionary; *ergo*, fire on the demonstrators; *ergo*. . . . At the end of this chain of thought I visualize you, my liberal friend, goose-stepping down Massachusetts Avenue in the uniform of an American Totalitarian Party in a mass rally where nothing but the most uproarious approval is manifest, except, by implication, on the part of silent and strangely scented clouds of smoke drifting over from the new "camps" where the "Negroes are living in retirement."

III.   How is Christianity involved in the Negro struggle? Dr. Martin Luther King has appealed to strictly Christian motives. He has based his non-violence on his belief that love can unite men, even enemies, in truth. That is to say that he has clearly spelled out the struggle for freedom not as a struggle for the Negro alone, but also for the white man. From the start, the non-violent element in the Negro struggle is oriented toward "healing" the sin of racism and toward unity in reconciliation. An absolutely necessary element in this reconciliation is that the white man should allow himself to learn the mute lesson which is addressed to him in the suffering, the non-violent protest, the loving acceptance of punishment for the violation of unjust laws, which the Negro freely and willingly brings down upon himself in the white man's presence, in the hope that the oppressor may come to see his own injustice.

The purpose of this suffering, freely sought and accepted in the spirit of Christ is the liberation of the Negro and the redemption of the white man, blinded by his endemic sin of racial injustice. In other words, the struggle for liberty is not merely regarded by this most significant sector of the Negro population, as a fight for political rights. It is this, and it is also much more. It is what Gandhi called *Satyagrāha*—a struggle first of all for the *truth,* outside and independent of specific political contingencies.

The mystique of Negro non-violence holds that the victory of truth is inevitable, but that the redemption of individuals is not inevitable. Though the truth will win, since in Christ it has already conquered, not everyone can "come to the light"—for if his works are darkness, he fears to let them be seen.

The Negro children of Birmingham, who walked calmly up to the police dogs that lunged at them with a fury capable of tearing their small bodies to pieces, were not only confronting the truth in an exalted moment of faith, a providential *kairos*. They were also in their simplicity, bearing heroic Christian witness to the truth, for they were exposing their bodies to death in order to show God and man that they believed in the just rights of their people, knew that those rights had been unjustly, shamefully and systematically violated, and realized that the violation called for expiation and redemptive protest, because it was an offense against God and His truth.

They were stating clearly that the time had come where such violations could no longer be tolerated. These Negro followers of Dr. King are convinced that there is more at stake than civil rights. They believe that the survival of America is itself in question. They believe that the sin of white America has reached such a proportion that it may call down a dreadful judgment, perhaps total destruction, on the whole country, unless atonement is made.

These Negroes are not simply judging the white man and rejecting him. On the contrary, they are seeking by Christian love and sacrifice to redeem him, to enlighten him, so as not only to save his soul from perdition, but also to awaken his mind and his conscience, and stir him to initiate the reform and renewal which may still be capable of saving our society. But this renewal must be the work of both the White and the Negro together. It cannot be planned and carried out by the white man alone or even by the Negro under the white man's paternal guidance. It demands some Negro initiative, and the white man cannot collaborate fruitfully until he recognizes the necessity of this initiative. The Negro is not going to be placated with assurances of respect and vague encouragement from our side. He is going to make sure that we are listening and that we have understood him, before he will believe in our attempts to help.

The purpose of non-violent protest, in its

deepest and most spiritual dimensions is then to awaken the conscience of the white man to the awful reality of his injustice and of his sin, so that he will be able to see that the Negro problem is really a *White* problem: that the cancer of injustice and hate which is eating white society and is only partly manifested in racial segregation with all its consequences, *is rooted in the heart of the white man himself.*

Only if the white man sees this will he be able to gradually understand the real nature of the problem and take steps to save himself and his society from complete ruin. As the Negro sees it, the Cold War and its fatal insanities are to a great extent generated within the purblind, guilt ridden, self-deceiving, self-tormenting and self-destructive psyche of the white man.

It is curious that while the Southern whites are surrounding their houses with floodlights, to protect themelves in case Negroes creep up to murder them in the dark, all the violence in the South to date has been on the part of the whites themselves. The tragic September bombings and shootings in Birmingham were a shocking contrast to the peace and dignity of the Washington March of August 28th. This was the white Southern reply to the March! Curious that the ones who repeatedly lecture the Negro on law and order, themselves are in league with murderers and thugs. Such "order" is no order at all, it is only organized injustice and violence. Barbara Deming, a white New England woman who demonstrated with the Negro children in Birmingham, was sent to jail with them. The jail was of course segregated. She was thrown in a cell full of white prostitutes and other delinquents, and found them not only furious and hostile towards her, but terrified lest the Negro children (who were still singing hymns after a sublime display of Christian heroism) might rape and murder them in the jail. Curious that these white Southerners (people to be pitied indeed) from their half-world of violence, petty thievery, vice and addiction, were the ones who felt themselves menaced, and menaced by the clear eyes of children! The truth is that they had very good reason to fear. The action of the children was aimed at them, and aimed directly at them. It was an attack not upon their property, their jobs, their social status, but upon their inmost conscience. And unless that attack could be met and deflected, *these people would not be able to continue as they were.*

In all literal truth, if they "heard" the message of the Negro children, they would cease to be the people they were. They would have to "die" to everything which was familiar and secure. They would have to die to their past, to their society with its prejudices and its inertia, die to its false beliefs, and *go over to the side of the Negroes*. For a Southern white, this would be a real "death."

Here is the radical challenge of Negro non-violence today. Here is why it is a source of uneasiness and fear to all white men who are attached to their security. If they are forced to listen to what the Negro is trying to say, the whites may have to admit that *their prosperity is rooted to some extent in injustice and in sin*. And, in consequence, this might lead to a complete re-examination of the political motives behind all our current policies, domestic and foreign, with the possible admission that we are wrong. Such an admission might, in fact, be so disastrous that its effects would dislocate our whole economy and ruin the country. These are not things that are consciously admitted, but they are confusedly present in our minds. They account for the passionate and mindless despera-tion with which we plunge this way and that, try-ing to evade the implications of our present crisis.

Certainly some such thoughts as these must underlie the apparent ambiguity in the Southern White's concept of "order." On a certain level, pathological if you like but none the less experien-tially real, Southern white society feels itself faced with destruction. It is menaced in its inmost be-ing, even though that "inmost being" is in fact only a spectre. But we know from experience with other notorious historical forms of fanaticism, that societies which "experience their reality" on this oniric and psychopathic level are precisely those whose members are most convinced of their own rightness, their own integrity, indeed their own complete infallibility. It is this experience of un-reality as real, and as something to be defended against objective facts and rights as though against the devil himself, that produces the inferno of racism and race conflict. The South is apparently in a state of perfect ripeness for this disastrous erup-tion of pathological hatreds and for all the fatal consequences that they bring with them. But the comparative sophistication of the North is no guarantee that the same evil is not present there, though perhaps in a more subtle form.

I have spoken of the ambiguity in the white Southern concept of "order." What is this? When in September of 1963 a cruel and senseless bomb-ing, too carefully planned and executed to have been the work of an ordinary group of criminals, destroyed a Baptist Church in Birmingham and killed four Negro children, Governor Wallace called out the National Guard to "keep order." The Negroes immediately appealed to President Kennedy to send United States troops to protect them against this local Alabama militia. It was evident to all that the White conception of "order" had nothing whatever to do with the protection of the rights of lives of Negroes. In the Southern

White mind the concept that a Negro might have rights in the same sense and in the same way as a white man simply does not exist. Hence the idea of "order" in the minds of people like Governor Wallace is simply that the Whites may be guaranteed safety in doing anything they like to the Negro without fear of retaliation. The function of the National Guard was purely and simply to ensure that the Negroes would not be able to fight back effectively after the bombing. In other words it was to "keep order" in much the same way that the SS kept order under Hitler.

And again, much like their Nazi prototypes, these militia-men are there perhaps also to *provoke* violence in order to have something concrete to "prevent." This is a slightly more subtle phenomenon that at first sight appears, because of the unanimous conviction of Southerners that the Negroes are really thirsting for white blood. This is the form, the only acceptable form, in which the Southern mind can face its own moral hazard. Subconsciously a vestigial Christian sense of guilt proclaims clearly the wrong that is being done and the remedies that are demanded. But this is filtered through into consciousness as a murderous threat to the symbolic "whiteness" which clothes the infantile Southern mind with its fixation on the mythical paradise before the Civil War. In fighting the Negro, the Southerner thinks he is fighting sin, death, the devil, Communism, immorality, lechery, hate, murder, hell itself. But what he is really fighting is the present.

For this reason the "fear of attack" represents in actual fact a very serious and earnest *desire to be attacked*. Not in order to be hurt, or to suffer, far from it: but in order to find the psychopathic myth verified, and all its practical conclusions justified. Therefore when the National Guard is called out to "keep order" it is recognized at least obscurely by all, both blacks and whites, that this act expresses an urgent and almost official need for disorder. It manifests a desire and a need bred by guilt, seeking to turn itself by every possible means into a self-fulfilling prophecy.

The *non-violent* and *religious* protest of the Negro against white racism and injustice is precisely what the Southern White (in his image of himself as upright and Christian) is least prepared to tolerate or to understand. It has to be seen as an obviously sinister cloak for Communist machinations. It has to be unmasked as pure malevolence, so that the appeal it aims at the white conscience may be discredited and ignored.

It has been said that Gandhian non-violence worked because it was aimed against a conscience that was still sensitive to an ethical appeal, and that it would never have worked against the Nazis. Is this a cliché, or is there some serious truth in it?

I think that if the Negroes' non-violent campaign continues in the South we will one day know, one way or the other.

There can be no question whatever that the mind of the average Southern White is not only unconsciously but even consciously and wilfully tending more and more to identify itself with an explicitly Nazi brand of racism.

Meanwhile, another significant fact must be mentioned. Not only have the local Southern police conspicuously refused to take any serious action in solving nearly fifty bombings that have recently taken place, some with loss of lives, in Southern states. The F.B.I. have also failed to produce any results. The arrival of Federal agents on the scene of violence is prompt and well publicized, but soon the whole affair is simply forgotten. It has been remarked that the F.B.I. shows far greater zeal in exercising its functions when dealing with organizations suspected of affiliation with Communism.

This conspicuous failure of the law to provide adequate protection or redress for Negroes subject to violent attack by Whites is having one very serious effect: it is causing Negroes to lose confidence in the efficacy of non-violence as a political tactic, because non-violence presupposes a basic respect for legality, and this is being completely destroyed by the inaction and hesitation of the

Federal Government, along with the belligerent contempt of law and justice on the part of some Southern states.

Unfortunately, not all Negroes can appreciate the Christian foundation of non-violent action as it is practised by the followers of Dr. King. Many northern Negro leaders, and especially the organizers of the Black Muslim movement, categorically reject Dr. King's ideas as sentimental. They believe that his non-violence is a masochistic exhibition of defeatism which flatters the whites, plays into their hands, and degrades the Negro still further by forcing him to submit uselessly to violence and humiliation. In some cases, the sharp criticism of Martin Luther King goes so far as to accuse him of deliberately and cynically sacrificing his followers in order to gain power and prestige for himself in white society.

This reaction against what is basically a Christian protest leads to another extreme: a black racism as intransigent and as fanatical as that of the white racists themselves. It is true that the Black Muslims must not be painted as a corporation of devils. Yet, the Muslim movement is one of absolutely hostile rejection of all that is white, including Christianity, conceived as the "white man's religion." Instead, Islam, regarded as "African religion" and as the worship of a "Black God" or at least of the Black Man's God, is substituted for it. Emphasis is laid on the martial and combative elements in the faith of Islam, and the first principle of all race relations is that the white man is never to be trusted. He is incapable of sincere, honest or humane actions. He is worthy only of hatred and contempt. No "dialogue" is possible between white and black, all that can be achieved is a complete separation. The Muslims' aim is to achieve this separation without violence, in so far as this may be possible: but they will not hesitate to use violence if this becomes necessary. Theoretically, then, the Black Muslims do not have a systematic program of violent attack on the white population, as some seem to imagine. But since the separation of which they dream is, and can be, no more than a dream, the tension between the races in the big cities of the north where the Muslims are concentrated, will most probably erupt in violence sooner or later. It can be said, however, that the fact that the Muslims are disciplined and organized makes them to some extent an asset: they will certainly try to control violence and direct it. This is preferable to completely uncontrolled and in some ways "uncaused" rioting, exploding at the slightest spark and spreading in aimless fury through whole cities until its force is spent. Yet the Muslims, however disciplined they themselves may be, can easily start a general conflagration.

The Black Muslims have so far had no influence in the south, and although the Negro spokesmen in the north are often hostile to Martin Luther King, he has immense prestige wherever Negroes are to be found in the United States, though Birmingham was not understood by all of them as a "victory" for their race. It seems, however, that all hope of really constructive and positive results from the Civil Rights Movement is to be placed in the Christian and non-violent elements. It is also possible that as the movement gains in power, the reasonableness and the Christian or at least ethical fervor of these elements will recede into the background and the Movement will become more and more an unreasoning and intransigeant mass movement dedicated to the conquest of sheer power, more and more inclined to violence.

If the Christian and non-violent element in Negro protest is finally discredited, it may mean that Christianity itself will become meaningless in Negro eyes. Those Negroes who attack the Christian leaders in the south are usually completely disillusioned with Christianity, if not bitterly hostile to it, because they are convinced that it has no other function than to keep the Negro in passive and helpless submission to his white oppressors. When white Christians express admiration and sympathy for Dr. King, this is immediately interpreted by his Negro critics as evidence of their own negative thesis.

As for the attitude of white Christians toward the Negro freedom movement, Protestants and Catholics alike are at best confused and evasive in their sympathies. One gets the impression that they mean well, and that they recognize the validity of the Negro's protest, but that they are so out of contact with the realities of the time that they have no idea how they can effectively help him. It is true that the American hierarchy has denounced the sin of racism. Here and there a Catholic bishop takes action to integrate his schools or to castigate the worst abuses of discrimination. Here and there Christian leaders get together to make encouraging statements. Yet at the same time, even those white Christians most favorable to the Negro cause, have been quick to react against the protests in Birmingham and Jackson, censuring them and demanding "more patience" on the Negro's part, sincerely believing that the whole problem can be adequately settled only by the administration in Washington. This, to the Negro, is more than naive. He cannot help but interpret it as evasion and bad faith, and consequently he has little or no confidence in *any* white Christian group including the Catholic Church.

Evidently, many white Christians will be

grieved and disappointed at this evaluation of their sincere concern over the Negro's struggle for his rights. They will remind the Negro that they *have* taken certain steps in his favor. They will expect him to be more grateful. I think the time has come to say two things about this attitude.

First of all, it shows that these well-meaning critics do not grasp the real dimensions of the problem as the Negro sees it. Like the average liberal, they think that the Negro is simply presenting a few reasonable demands which can be met by legislative action. And, as a corollary to this, they assume that if the Negro were to ask any more than this, he would be unreasonable if not rebellious.

In actual fact the Negro is not simply asking to be "accepted into" the white man's society, and eventually "absorbed by it," so that race relations in the U.S. may finally come to be something like those in Latin America. I think that most Catholics tend, half consciously, to imagine that this would be a reasonable outcome: let the United States imitate those countries that were settled by Catholics in the first place, and where there has never been a very strict color line. Catholic values will triumph and there will be no more racial problems, because the United States will be like Brazil.

As present events in Brazil make quite clear, this is no solution.

The actions and attitudes of white Christians all, without exception, contain a basic and axiomatic assumption of white superiority, even when the pleas of the Negro for equal rights are hailed with the greatest benevolence. It is simply taken for granted that, since the white man is superior, the *Negro wants to become a white man*. And we, liberals and Christians that we are, advance generously, with open arms, to embrace our little black brother and welcome him into white society.

The Negro is not only not grateful, he is not even impressed. In fact, he shows by his attitude that he is at the same time antagonized and disgusted by our stupidity. This antagonism will be all the stronger in proportion as he has had to struggle heroically to deliver himself from the incubus of inferiority feelings. And here, I think, is where all Christians, including Catholics are, innocently no doubt, doing the gravest harm to Christian truth.

For some unknown reason, the white man (especially the Southern white) does not seem to realize that he has been rather closely observed, for the last two centuries, by his Negro slaves, servants, share-croppers, concubines, and bastards. He does not seem to be aware of the fact that they know a great deal about him, and, in fact, understand him in some ways better than he understands himself. This information has never been passed on to the white man, who has never dreamed of asking for it. He has assumed that the ideas of the Negro were more or less worthless in the first place. Do Negroes think? Of course not: they just sing, dance, make love, and lie in the shade doing nothing, because they are *different*. They haven't got the energy to think!

The Negro knows precisely why the white man imagines that the Negro wants to be a White Man. The White Man is too insecure in his fatuous self-complacency to be able to imagine anything else.

Consequently, when the Catholic Church gives the impression that it regards the South as a vast potential pool of "Negro converts" in which a zealous and ardent white apostolate can transform a few million Uncle Toms into reasonably respectable imitations of white Catholics, this actually does very little to make the Negro respect the truth of Christ, practically nothing to help him understand the mystery of Christ in His Church. Especially when he observes that the converted Negro is still not welcome in every southern Catholic Church and even where he is admitted at all, he may only receive Communion *after* all the Whites.

It is often quite evident that the genuinely

warm sympathy which so many Catholics have
for the Negro is nevertheless something the Negro
himself now accepts only with resignation and
disillusionment. What we love in the Negro tends
to be, once again, the same old image of the vaude-
ville darkie, the quaint Black Mammy of planta-
tion days, the Pullman porter with ready wit, the
devoted retainer whose whole family has served a
white Southern feudal tribe for generations. This
is a caricature of the Negro of which the Negro
himself has long since grown tired, and its chief
function is to flatter the white man's sense of
superiority.

One has yet to find very many Catholics, including priests, who are really able to deal with
Negroes on an equal footing, that is to say without the specious and fraudulent mediation of this
image. Most of us are congenitally unable to think
black, and yet that is precisely what we must do
before we can even hope to understand the crisis in
which we find ourselves. Our best considered and
most sympathetic consideration of the Negro's
plight is one calculated to antagonize him because
it reflects such pitiful inability to *see* him, right
before our nose, as a real human being and not as
a higher type of domestic animal. Furthermore we
do not bother really to listen to what he says, because we assume that when the dialogue really
begins, he will already be thinking just like our-

selves. And in the meantime we are not too disposed to offend the white racists, either. We still
want to please everybody with soft words and
pleasant generalizations, which we convince ourselves are necessary for "charity." Is it charity to
leave the racists sunk in a sin that cries out to
heaven for vengeance?

A genuinely Catholic approach to the Negro
would assume not only that the White and the
Negro are essentially equal in dignity (and this, I
think, we do generally assume) but also that they
are brothers in the fullest sense of the word. This
means to say that a genuinely Catholic attitude in
matters of race is one which concretely accepts and
fully recognizes the fact that different races and
cultures are *correlative*. *They mutually complete
one another*. The white man needs the Negro,
and needs to know that he needs him.

White calls for black just as black calls for
white. Our significance as white men is to be seen
entirely in the fact that all men are not white. Until this fact is grasped, we will never realize our
true place in the world, and we will never achieve
what we are meant to achieve in it. The white
man is *for* the black man: that is why he is white.
The black man is for the white man: that is why
he is black. But so far, we have managed only to
see those relationships in a very unsatisfactory and
distorted fashion.

First of all, there was the crude initial concept: the black man was *for* the white man, in the sense that he belonged to him as his slave. But in the relationship of master and slave there is no correlative responsibility. The master is like God, who cannot enter into a relationship with a creature: the creature can only enter into a relationship with Him. So the master could do what he liked with the slave, and perhaps, incidentally, he might find himself, without realizing it, living to some extent *for* the slave whom he had come to trust and love. But though there was a germinating humanity in this "relationship," there was no sense of a real social obligation to slaves as such, who therefore were never really admitted to be human beings. Thus though the south of slavery days was a kind of Eden for the white man (and is still remembered in the collective southern myth as Eden), it was without human significance because it was empty of basic truth: the truth of *Man* was absent, because here were two different kinds of men who were supposed, in the order of nature, to complete one another as correlatives, and one of them was not admitted to human status.

The Civil War came, and the Negro acquired a human status on the books of law: but only on the books. In actual fact his position gradually became even less human than before.

To assume the superiority of the white race and

of European-American culture as axiomatic, and to proceed from there to "integrate" all other races and cultures by a purely one-sided operation is a pure travesty of Catholic unity in truth. In fact, this fake Catholicism, this parody of unity which is no unity at all but a one-sided and arbitrary attempt to reduce others to a condition of identity with ourselves, is one of the most disastrous of misconceptions.

It may be true that a French missionary who brings the truth of the Gospel to a West African pagan is bringing him the truth indeed. But unfortunately, the fatal tendency has too often been to assume that *everything* he was bringing, down to his clothes, his table manners, his Cartesian habits of thought, his Gallic self-esteem and in a word, the infallibility of the *bien pensant* were all pure revelations of God and His Church. In such conditions, missionaries have assumed, with extreme generosity, that their only function was to *give* of their sublime fulness, and that it was never necessary for them to receive, to learn, to accept any kind of a spiritual gift from the native and from his indigenous culture. Material contributions—yes. But nothing else. There has generally been no conception at all that the white man had anything to learn from the Negro. And now, the irony is that the Negro (especially the Christian Negro of the heroic stamp of Dr. King) *is offering*

*the white man a "message of salvation," but the
white man is so blinded by his self-sufficiency and
self-conceit that he does not recognize the peril in
which he puts himself by ignoring the offer.*

Is the white man really in a position to recognize the providential character of this hour? If I
say that the Negro offers him an "opportunity,"
the white man will perhaps scrutinize him afresh
in order to find out what he has to sell. And what
will he see? Something at once disturbing and un-
attractive. Processions of discontented black men
and women carrying signs. Groups of exalted children singing hymns. Frightened but determined
people letting themselves be rolled around the
street by the power of firehoses. There is determination there, no doubt; they obviously mean
business. But we have determination too, and
there is no need at all for us to have the hoses
turned on us.

This is not the point. The Negro, in fact, has
nothing to sell. He is only offering us the occasion
*to enter with him into a providential reciprocity
willed for us by God.* He is inviting us to understand him as necessary to our own lives, and as
completing them. He is warning us that we cannot do without him, and that if we insist on regarding him as an enemy, an object of contempt,
or a rival, we will perhaps sterilize and ruin our
own lives. He is telling us that unless we can enter

into a vital and Christian relationship with him, there will be hate, violence and civil war indeed: and from this violence perhaps none of us will emerge whole.

It must then be said that this most critical moment in American history is the providential "hour," the *kairos* not merely of the Negro, but of the white man. It is, or at any rate it can be, God's hour. It can be the hour of vocation, the moment in which, hearing and understanding the will of God as expressed in the urgent need of our Negro brother, we can respond to that inscrutable will in a faith that faces the need of reform and creative change, in order that the demands of truth and justice may not go unfulfilled.

It is for this reason that the "prudence" and the (self-styled) wisdom of some white Christian leaders may well prove to be a sign of spiritual blindness, and as such it may be decisive in leading the Negro away from Christian truth and natural reason, to embark on a violent and chaotic fight for power characterized only by brutality and pragmatism. In this struggle the lessons given by the white police and politicians in the South will certainly be turned to good advantage.

What the Negro now seeks and expects (or perhaps what he has entirely given up expecting) from the white Christian is not sermons on patience, but a creative and enlightened understanding of his effort to meet the demands of God in this, his *kairos*. What he expects of us is some indication that we are capable of seeing a little of the vision he has seen, and of sharing his risks and his courage. What he asks us is not the same old string of meaningless platitudes that we have always offered him in lieu of advice. He asks us to listen to him, and to pay some attention to what *he* has to say. He seriously demands that we learn something from him, because he is convinced that we need this, and need it badly.

Negro writers, like James Baldwin, have repeatedly demonstrated that this conviction lends an extraordinary power to their words. There is no question that they have more to say than anybody else writing in America today. Many have read their books and heard their message, but few are prepared to understand it because they simply cannot conceive of a white man learning anything worth while from a Negro. Still less can they imagine that the Negro might quite possibly have a prophetic message from God to the society of our time.

In simple terms, I would say that the message is this: white society has sinned in many ways. It has betrayed Christ by its injustices to races it considered "inferior" and to countries which it colonized. In particular it has sinned against Christ in its lamentable injustices and cruelties to the

Negro. The time has come when both White and Negro have been granted, by God, a unique and momentous opportunity to repair this injustice and to reestablish the violated moral and social order on a new plane.

We have this opportunity because the Negro has taken the steps which made it possible. He has refused to accept the iniquity and injustice of white discrimination. He has seen that to acquiesce in this injustice is no virtue, but only collaboration in evil. He has declared that he rejects both the physical evil of segregation and the moral evil of passive acquiescence in the white man's sin. But this is only the beginning. Now the white man must do his share, or the Negro's efforts will have no fruit.

The sin of the white man is to be expiated, through *a genuine response to the redemptive love of the Negro for him*. The Negro is ready to suffer, if necessary to die, if this will make the white man understand his sin, repent of it, and atone for it. But this atonement must consist of two things:

1) A complete reform of the social system which permits and breeds such injustices.

2) This work of reorganization must be carried out under the inspiration of the Negro whose providential time has now arrived, and who has received from God enough light, ardor and spirit-

ual strength to free the white man in freeing himself from the white man.

I state these two conditions as nakedly and un-equivocally as I find them in the words of Negro leaders. My only comment is that in making these demands, they are committing themselves very heavily to provide answers, in case we should ever ask them any questions. The Negro is saying that in effect *he has answers*. So far, his actions at Birmingham make his claim credible. I, for one, am willing to hear more. But I must admit there is as yet a certain vagueness in the inconclusive remarks so far advanced concerning the future. I am not too sure the Negro knows, any better than anyone else, where this country is actually going.

Yet this is a challenge and a very bold one. The Negro leaders are making some fantastic claims. And they are perhaps all the more fantastic be-cause those who make them have half despaired of ever being heard. Certainly, all the official good will of the Administration is in no sense an ac-knowledgement that these claims have ever been considered in their depth. That is because Wash-ington is professionally capable only of seeing this as a political issue. Actually, it is a spiritual and religious one, and this element is by far the most important. But it is the element that no one is ready to see.

A white detective in Birmingham, watching

the children file by the score into the paddy wag-
ons, gave expression to the mind of the nation
when he said: "If this is religion, I don't want any
part of it!" If this is really what the mind of white
America has concluded, then we stand judged by
our own thought.

What is demanded of us is not necessarily that
we believe that the Negro has mysterious and
magic answers in the realm of politics and social
control, *but that his spiritual insight into our common crisis is something we must take seriously.*

By and large, in the midst of the clamor of
every possible kind of jaded and laughable false
prophet, the voice of the American Negro has in it
a genuine prophetic ring. Who knows if we will
ever get another chance to hear it?

In any case the Negro demands that his conditions be met with full attention and seriousness.
The white man may not fully succeed in this—
but he must at least try with all the earnestness at
his command. Otherwise, the moment of grace
will pass without effect. The merciful *kairos* of
truth will turn into the dark hour of destruction
and hate. The awakened Negro will forget his
moment of Christian hope and Christian inspiration. He will deliberately drive out of his heart the
merciful love of Christ. He will no longer be the
gentle, wide-eyed child singing hymns while police dogs lunge at his throat. There will be no

more hymns and no more prayer vigils. He will become a Samson whose African strength flows ominously back into his arms. He will suddenly pull the pillars of white society crashing down upon himself and his oppressor. And perhaps, somewhere, out of the ruins, a new world (a black world) will one day arise.

This is the "message" which the Negro is trying to give white America. I have spelled it out for myself, subject to correction, in order to see whether a white man is even capable of grasping the words, let alone believing them. For the rest, you have Moses and the Prophets: Martin Luther King, James Baldwin and the others. Read them, and see for yourself what they are saying.

IV.   It is related that when Mohammed was seeking the light, he thought of
becoming a Christian. He went to some Nestorian
Christians in a corner of Arabia, and sought a sign
of the truth of Christianity from them. In order
to see whether they had faith, he asked them to
show him the credibility of the Christian message
by walking barefoot on red hot coals. The Nes-
torians told him that he was mad. Mohammed,
saying nothing, departed from them. And soon
the conviction that he sought came to him in the
burning heat of the Arabian desert. It was a truth
of stark and dreadful simplicity—to be proved by
the sword.

THE LEGEND
OF TUCKER CALIBAN

The deep elemental stirrings that lead to social change, begin within the hearts of men whose thoughts have hitherto not been articulate or who have never gained a hearing, and whose needs are therefore ignored, suppressed, and treated as if they did not exist. There is no revolution without a voice. The passion of the oppressed must first of all make itself heard at least among themselves, in spite of the insistence of the privileged oppressor that such needs cannot be real, or just, or urgent. The more the cry of the oppressed is ignored, the more it strengthens itself with a mysterious power that is to be gained from myth, symbol and prophecy. There is no revolution without poets who are also seers. There is no revolution without prophetic songs.

The voice of the American Negro began to be heard long ago, even in the days of his enslavement. He sang of the great mysteries of the Old

Testament, the *magnalia Dei* which are at the heart of the Christian liturgy. In a perfect, unconscious and spontaneous spirit of prayer and prophecy, the Negro spirituals of the last century remain as classic examples of what a living liturgical hymnody ought to be, and how it comes into being: not in the study of the research worker or in the monastery library, still less in the halls of curial offices, but where men suffer oppression, where they are deprived of identity, where their lives are robbed of meaning, and where the desire of freedom and the imperative demand of truth forces them to give it meaning: a religious meaning. Such religion is not the "opium of the people," but a prophetic fire of love and courage, fanned by the breathing of the Spirit of God who speaks to the heart of His children in order to lead them out of bondage. Hence the numinous force of the great and primitive art of the American Negro, a force which makes itself felt precisely where men have lost the habit of looking for "art," for instance in that potent and mysterious jazz which has kept alive the inspiration of the traditional "blues," the contemporary voice of the American Negro. And also in the "Freedom Songs" which he now sings, in the Baptist Churches of the South where he prepares to march out and face the police of states, already frankly Fascist and racist, which arm themselves against him with clubs, fire hoses, police dogs and electric cattle prods, throwing their jails wide-open to receive him. His song continues to resound in prison like the songs of Paul and his companions, in the Acts of the Apostles.

The Negro novelist and essayist has an important part in this creative expression of the present sense of *kairos* which is behind the great drive for "Freedom Now." We remember of course Richard Wright, whose warm voice is now silent, but who speaks still in his followers. We think especially of James Baldwin, who ranks with Martin Luther King as one of the most influential of Negro spokesmen today. *Go Tell it on the Mountain* is at once Baldwin's first novel and his best, as well as the one which has the most to say about the motives and the spirit of the Black Revolution in America. His hard-hitting tract, *The Fire Next Time,* which borrows its title from one of the Negro spirituals and which has an eschatological reference, is a manifesto of the Negro freedom movement which has done more than anything else to shock white readers into recognizing the seriousness and the unfamiliarity of the situation which they have been more or less taking for granted.

The title of the first novel of William Melvin Kelley, *A Different Drummer,* is taken significantly from Henry Thoreau. Thoreau, the hermit and a prophet of non-violence, preached civil disobedience in protest against unjust laws a century ago, before the Civil War. He was an early champion of Negro freedom as well as a notorious nonconformist who seems to have believed that the American revolution had either misfired or had never really taken place. Thoreau said: "If a man does not keep pace with his companions, perhaps it is because he hears a different drummer. Let him step to the music he hears, however measured or far away." It is an admirable title for the most mythical and in some sense the most prophetic of the Negro novels: one which makes quite clear the fact that the Negro hears a drummer with a totally different beat, and one which the white man is not yet capable of understanding. Yet it is imperative for him to pay attention. The trite and nasal hillbilly fiddling to which the white American mind continues its optimistic jig, has long ago ceased to have a meaning, and the "most advanced country in the world" runs the risk of being, in certain crucial matters, precisely the most retarded. Certainly there is great risk for a nation which is still playing cowboys and Indians in its own imagination—but with H-bombs and Polaris submarines at its disposal!

A Different Drummer is more than a brilliant first novel by a young Negro writer. It is a parable which spells out some of the deep spiritual implications of the Negro battle for full civic rights in the

United States and for a completely human status in the world today. This is more than a story of Negro protest; it is a myth endowed with extraordinary creative power bringing to light the providential significance of a tragedy in which, whether we know it or not, understand it or not, like it or not, we are all playing a part. Since we are all in the struggle, we might as well try to find out what it really means. The works of Negro writers are there to tell us. Such books cannot be ignored. They must be read with deep attention. They spell out a message of vital importance, which is not to be found anywhere else at the present moment, and on the acceptance of which the survival of American freedom may depend.

The book opens as the loafers on the porch of a general store, in a small town of the deep South, watch a truckload of rock salt pass through on its way to the farm of a Negro called Tucker Caliban. It ends as the same loafers, after watching all the Negroes, mysteriously and without explanation, clear out of the state, lynch the last Negro available to them, a potentate from the North, and founder of a black racist movement.

The heart of the story is the sense of *kairos*, the realization that the Negro's hour of destiny has struck. No one can deny that this is one of the most striking and mysterious characteristics of the Negro freedom movement. It is this sense which awakening everywhere in the Negro masses of the South, especially in the youth, has brought them by the hundreds and thousands out of the ghettoes in which they have vegetated for a century of frustrated and despairing expectation. It is this that has moved them to action, not so much because a few inspired leaders like Martin Luther King have called them to action, but because the entire Negro race, and all the vast majority of "Colored races" all over the world, have suddenly and spontaneously become conscious of their real power and, it seems of a destiny that is all their own. Hence, inseparable from the sense of *kairos* is a conviction of *vocation,* of a providential role to play in the world of our time. With the awakening of independence in Africa the American Negro has become acutely conscious of his own underprivileged status, and of his yearning not only to become a "part of White Society" (for this is now evidently a doubtful benefit in his eyes) but to play his own creative role in human history. One finds everywhere in American Negro society a more or less explicit anticipation of the end of the white domination of the world and the decline of European-American civilization. The Negro therefore cannot be content merely to be integrated into something he regards as already over and done with. And this is what the myth in Kelley's novel is all about.

Tucker Caliban is the central figure in the

myth. He is the New Negro. The completely new
Negro: not the Negro organizer from the North,
not the Negro who has been to college, but a kind
of preternatural figure, the lineal descendant of a
giant African chief who came over with his tribe
in a slave ship to be bought—and killed—by the
first Governor of the mythical southern state in
which the story takes place. The giant "African"
is the symbol of the Negro race and of its innate
spirit, which the white man has tried first to tame
for his own purposes, then to destroy. Tucker
Caliban is not giant. He is a small, intense, taci-
turn Negro, aligned with no group, no movement
and no cause. The implication is that he sees completely through even the best of movements and
of causes. He also understands the problems of
white people. He views them completely objectively and without bitterness. He harbors no delu-
sions about them, and he places no hope whatever
in the official benevolence of the white man. His is
the spirit in which the Negro freedom movement
must develop. In him the wisdom and strength of
the African ancestor must one day awaken.

Meanwhile, the Calibans have served the family of the Governor for over a century both as slaves
and as freedmen. Tucker's father is the typical of
the venerable Negro servant, loyal and entirely devoted to his master, in other words, he is what the
Negroes now regard with deepest scorn: he is an

"Uncle Tom," or one who has fully accepted an inferior position in white society.

Tucker, without hatred and without rebellion, driven by an inner force which he does not quite understand himself and which baffles everybody who comes in contact with him, first buys a piece of land from the family his family has served so long. Then he leaves their service, and farms his newly acquired land for about a year. Finally, following inscrutable interior messages, he sterilizes his field with rock salt, shoots his mule and his cow, sets fire to his house, and leaves in the night with his pregnant wife. He simply vanishes.

At this, all the Negroes in the state begin to leave. It is not necessary to know where they go. They just go. Out of the state, out of the south. In a few days they are all gone, leaving empty houses which they have not bothered to sell, with the doors wide open, furniture inside.

Their departure is a symbolic statement: it is the final refusal to accept paternalism, tutelage, and all different forms of moral, economic, psychological and social servitude wished on them by the whites. In the last analysis, it is the final rejection of the view of life implied by white culture. It is a definitive "NO" to White America.

The book is about the bewilderment with which this is observed and dimly understood by all the people who see them go: the poor whites, the

child of a white sharecropper, the descendants of
the first Governor, Southerners educated in the
north, and finally the Rev. Bennett Bradshaw,
founder of the Black Jesuits, a Northern Negro
Leader who is just as mystified as everyone else by
the things that are happening. Though he, more
than anyone, would have wanted to set all these
things in motion, he has never been consulted or
even dreamed of. He is not wanted any more than
the benevolent white liberal is wanted, because he
has no real power to do anything, to start anything, to move anyone. Yet for the Southern
Whites there has to be some explanation that fits
their picture of life, and reassures them that things
are what the South has always believed them to
be. In a final tragic irony, the loafers at the store
follow the irresponsible inspiration of one of their
number and blame the Black Jesuit for engineer-
ing the hegira. After beating him up they drive
him in his own Cadillac to Tucker Caliban's
gutted farm and his screams in the Southern night
ring down the curtain on this strange morality
play about the evil of our time.

Evil is the word! Those who have seen, at first
hand, the eerie glow in the eyes of the racist, those
who have heard their peculiar silences as they
stand together in the shadows waiting for the
forces within them to reach some mysterious point
where inner confusion and self-hate turn into vio-

lent fury—those who have seen this are aware of what it means to see apparently good and harmless men possessed with an evil so total and so complete that they prefer not to understand it, or refer to it, or treat it as if it existed.

Yet this evil is not something purely and simply confined to "white trash" in the South. What is open and expressed in the South may perhaps be hidden and implicit everywhere in the nation that is so fascinated with violence and with the myth of power that it seems to have lost interest in anything else—with the possible exception of sex.

There is no need to intone a litany of clichés in a useless attempt to convey some idea of the power with which this story is told. It is a power without the bitterness and frustration that give such bite to the works of James Baldwin. Kelley, a northern Negro like Baldwin, is much more tranquil and reflective. The force of the myth itself seems to have absorbed and tamed the bitter rage that might have gone into such a story. There is no rage. Resentment is sublimated into irony. This accounts for the book's unforgettable impact. The myth of Tucker Caliban tells the same kind of truth as dreams tell us in our moments of personal crisis, spelling out to us in symbols, ranging from idyll to hallucination and to nightmare, the truths that are struggling for acceptance and for expression in our hearts.

That is the particular value of such a book. It gives us a message which, like all prophetic messages, is mostly in code so that we can both hear and not hear, we can accept just as much of it as we are able. But if we really want to, we can understand completely. What, then, is the message?

The message of this book is very much the same as that which we read in James Baldwin's *The Fire Next Time* (written and published after *A Different Drummer*). It is the same message which the best American Negro writers are now, with a rather astonishing unanimity and confidence, announcing to the white world as their diagnosis of that world's sickness, with their suggestions for escaping the death which is otherwise inevitable.

First of all, we must seriously face the magnanimity of the statement. It would be all too easy for the Negroes simply to write the Whites off as a total loss (as indeed the Black Muslims are doing) and be done with them forever. This solution is appealing not only in its simplicity, but also in its correspondence with the deepest psychological need of the Negro, the need to recover his belief in his own autonomous reality, the need to get the white man, spiritually and psychologically, off his back. But in point of fact, such a solution is not really possible, as the best Negro writers see quite clearly. They have certainly rejected, with all their force, the gross and subtle forms of alienation imposed on them by white society, even where it claims to do most to make them "free." But the thing that so many readers have failed to see in these books is the rather convincing assurance that there is one *kairos* for everybody. The time that has providentially come for the black man is also providential for the white man.

This implies a profoundly Christian understanding of man's freedom in history—a point that must be underscored.

The Negro revolution is a real revolution, and it is definitely not Marxian. It may have some very violent and destructive potentialities in it, but they have nothing to do with Soviet Communism. To identify the Negro freedom movement as a Red-inspired revolt against western democracy is a totally ludicrous evasion, and one which involves complete and incurable ignorance of what is actually happening. This is of course precisely why it is accepted with total satisfaction by the entire South. In Alabama, Mississippi, Georgia, Louisiana, it is an article of faith that "all this trouble with the Nigras" has been fomented by Communist agents.

Though writers like Baldwin and doubtless Kelley lay no claim to be Christians, their view is still deeply Christian and implies a substantially Christian faith in the spiritual dynamism with which man freely creates his own history, not as an autonomous and titanic self-affirmation, but in obedience to the mystery of love and freedom at work under the surface of human events.

In the light of this, then, the hour of freedom is seen also as an hour of salvation. But it is not an hour of salvation for the Negro only. The white man, if he can possibly open the ears of his heart and listen intently enough to hear what the Negro is now hearing, can recognize that he is himself called to freedom and to salvation in the same *kairos* of events which he is now, in so many different ways, opposing or resisting.

These books tell us that it is the Negro who hears or believes he hears, the true voice of God in history, and interprets it rightly. The white man has lost his power to hear any inner voice other than that of his own demon who urges him to preserve the *status quo* at any price, however desperate, however iniquitous and however cruel. The white man's readiness to destroy the world rather than change it is dictated by this inner demon, which he cannot recognize, but which the Negro clearly identifies.

The tragedy of the present crisis in race relations (say the Negro writers) is therefore essentially the white man's tragedy, and he will destroy himself unless he can understand and undergo the *metanoia* that will bring him into harmony with the awakened forces that are being revealed to him in the struggle of his black brother. The Negro may have much to suffer, and the times ahead may yet prove most terrible: but essentially, for him, the days of tragedy are over. He has awakened and taken his destiny into his own hands.

Tucker Caliban, when he burned his house down and took off into the night, was not a "tragic" hero. On the contrary, the implication of tragedy is all affixed to the comfortable and secure life which his father led as a loyal servant of the white Governor's family. Tragedy is not in freedom but in moral servitude. We are no longer in the world of Aeschylus and Sophocles in which the aspiration to freedom is linked with unbearable guilt and punished by the gods. We are in a Christian world in which man is redeemed, liberated from guilt by the inner truth that makes him free to obey the Lord of History. It is the Lord of History who demands of the Negro a complete break with his past servitudes. And the break must be made by the Negro himself, without any need of the white man's paternalistic approval. It is absolutely necessary for the Negro to dissolve all bonds that hold him, like a navel cord, in passive dependence on the good pleasure of the white man's society.

The real tragedy is that of the white man who

does not realize that though he seems to himself to be free, he is actually the victim of the same servitudes which he has imposed on the Negro: passive subjection to the lotus-eating commercial society that he has tried to create for himself, and which is shot through with falsity and unfreedom from top to bottom. He makes a great deal of fuss about "individual freedom," but one may ask if such freedom really exists. Is there really a genuine freedom for the person or only the irresponsibility of the atomized individual members of mass society?

The presence of the Negro in a state of humiliation and dependence may serve, perhaps to perpetuate the illusion of power and autonomy which the white loafers on the porch of the village store imagine they enjoy. Actually, their own lives are empty, pointless, absurd, totally lacking in freedom. The departure of the Negroes suddenly makes that truth inescapable. Hence the frustrated whites confront the meaninglessness of their world. They know no other way of "facing" such facts than violence.

This, then, according to our Negro writers, is the plight of the white American and indeed of the whole western world. Europe cannot save face by sitting back complacently and viewing with pity the conflicts and confusions of white America. When the house next door is on fire you too are in danger. America does not stand judgment alone. It is the whole white world, including Russia, that stands accused of centuries of injustice, prejudice and racism. All white men together, in spite of their fantasies of innocence, are prisoners of the same illusion, seduced by their own slogans, obsessed by the voice of an inner demon. They have no better alternatives than the passivities and oral fantasies of the consumer's dream-world and the violent barbarities with which they react, when briefly awakened, to all that threatens to contradict their infantile dream.

In such a situation, it is absurd for the Negro to place any hope either in the white Liberal or in the affluent Negro Leader. Though there may be, in each of these cases some awareness of the problem, the awareness is not deep enough to mean anything. On the contrary, it only makes matters worse by bringing a new element of delusion into the minds of those concerned. The Liberal and the Negro Leader are, each in his own way, completely committed to the comforts and securities and therefore to the falsities of the *status quo*. Each in his own way has sold out to the establishment. And his defection is all the more vicious because, with his seeming awareness of the problems and his demonstrations of great good will, he only encourages the Negro to continue in hapless submission, to "wait" and to hope for that same magic solution which continues, as always before, to recede further into the future.

To neither of these, says Kelley, can the Negro profitably or even safely listen. The most pitiful character in the book is perhaps the Southern white liberal who was once a promising young radical writer and crusader in the halcyon days of the thirties, but who allowed himself to be intimidated and silenced, in order to protect his family. His life thereafter is doomed to sterility, impotence, uselessness. He may be prosperous and secure, but he is a total failure. He has betrayed his truth and his vocation, and is therefore miserable.

This comes close to being a standard formula in the new Negro literature. It calls white society before the bar of history and hands down the judgment that it has lamentably failed. Christianity itself is prominently associated in the failure. Without delaying here to make certain distinctions and to defend the basic truth of Christianity we must admit that the judgment is not altogether without foundation. The practical conduct of many Christians, of whole groups and entire "churches," lends it a great deal of support. Christians have perhaps too often been content to delude themselves with vague slogans and abstract formulas about brotherly love. They have too easily become addicted to token gestures of good will and "charity" which they have then taken as a total dispensation from all meaningful action and genuine concern in the crucial problems of our time. As a result they have become unable to listen to the voice of God in the events of the time, and have resisted that voice instead of obeying it.

What is the conclusion? The white man is so far gone that he cannot free the Negro because he cannot even free himself. Hence these books are not in any sense demanding that the whites now finally free the Negroes. On the contrary, the magnificent paradox they utter is that the Negro has a mission to free the white man: and he can begin to do this if he learns to free himself. His first step to freedom must be the clear realization that he cannot depend on the white man or trust him for anything, since the white man is hopelessly impotent, deluded and stupefied by his own alienation.

Such is the "message" of the Negro to white America, delivered by men who, to my mind, are the most impressive and inspired writers in our country today. Is the message "true"?

I must say that messages like this cannot be clearly declared to be either "true" or "false" until time itself lays out all the evidence before us. But that is precisely our difficulty. We cannot wait. We have to decide *now*, before the truth or falsity of the message becomes evident. We have to be willing to make it evident.

The question is, then, not whether the message is true, but whether it is *credible*. And to this I can only give the answer of one man's opinion. Comparing the spiritual earnestness of the message, the creative vitality of the messengers, the fruits of the message, with all the fumbling evasions and inanities of those who disbelieve the message, I can come up with no better choice than to listen very seriously to the Negro, and what he has to say. I for one, am absolutely ready to believe that *we need him to be free, for our sake even more than for his own.*

The school children of Birmingham would have convinced me, if I had not been already convinced. I find the message entirely credible. Doubtless, it may not be infallibly true, but I think there is no hope for us unless we are able to take seriously the obvious elements of truth which it contains.

PART TWO

The Diaspora

THE CHRISTIAN IN WORLD CRISIS:
REFLECTIONS ON THE MORAL
CLIMATE OF THE 1960's

"We feel it our duty to beseech men, especially those who have the responsibility of public affairs, to spare no pain or effort until world events follow a course in keeping with man's destiny and dignity . . . Nevertheless, unfortunately the law of fear still reigns among peoples . . . There is reason to hope, however, that by meeting and negotiating men may come to discover that one of the most profound requirements of their nature is this: between them and their respective peoples it is not fear that should reign, but love—a love that tends to express itself in collaboration."

JOHN XXIII, *Pacem in Terris.*

I. CAN WE CHOOSE PEACE?

A man is said to be "responsible" in so far as he is able to give a rational and humanly satisfactory answer, or "response," concerning his acts and the motives behind them. Cain, for instance, after the murder of Abel, was asked where Abel was—a question of primordial and typological importance. Cain's answer was not clear.

In discussing the fateful problems of violence, hatred and power politics in terms of Christian responsibility, we must first discover what question is being asked of us, and by whom. If we are willing to face the question along with the questioner, we may eventually become able to give a true and clear answer.

The question is not merely, "Where is our violent and overstimulated culture leading us?" or "Can total war be avoided?" or "Will the Communists take over the West?" or "Will the West win the cold war?" or "Will the survivors of a nuclear war envy the dead?" From the standpoint of the present essay, such questions are irrelevant. Not that the issues they raise may not be vitally important, but the surmises and conjectures which might be offered as answers to such questions are really not answers to anything. They are beguiling guesses which seek to allay anxiety and which may well threaten to misdirect our best efforts if not to justify actions of which we ought to be ashamed.

The more important question is not "What is going to happen to us?" but "What are we going to do?'' or more cogently, *"What are our real intentions?"* This last question is probably seldom asked with sufficient seriousness. Let us suppose it is not simply something we ask ourselves. Let us hear it as a question that is proposed to us by the Lord and Judge of life and death. Let us bear in mind another such question: "Friend, whereto art thou come?" (Matthew 26:50.) Judas, somewhat subtler and far unhappier than Cain, having learned some fundamental truths, happened to know that the acceptable answer to such crucial questions had something to do with love. So he kissed Christ. But his kiss was a sign of betrayal.

We are being asked the very same question, if not directly and openly by Christ, at least by history of which we, as Christians, believe Him to be the Lord. I do not say that our love of Christ, desperate and confused as it is, is little more than a gesture of betrayal. But let us be sincere about facing the question, and hope, through God's grace, to answer it better than Judas.

Quite apart from what the Communists may or may not do, what are we, the dwindling and confused Christian minority in the West, going to do? Or at least, what do we *really want to do?* Do we intend to settle our problems peacefully or by force? Have we anything left to say about it at all? Have not the decisions been taken, to a great extent, out of our hands? Not yet. Among our leaders, some are Christians. Others cling to humanitarian principles which should be relevant here. These leaders will (we hope) take kindly to suggestions and to pleas that are based on Christian ethical norms. We have been very close to nuclear war, more than once, in the past five years. Has disaster been avoided merely by a healthy fear of the bomb, or have more humane and rational motives come to our aid?

The Christian is not only bound to avoid certain evils, but he is responsible for very great goods. This is often forgotten. The doctrine of the Incarnation leaves the Christian obligated at once to God and to man. If God has become man, then no Christian is ever allowed to be indifferent to man's fate. Whoever believes that Christ is the Word made flesh believes that every man must in some sense be regarded as Christ. For all are at least potentially members of the Mystical Christ. Who can say with absolute certainty of any other man that Christ does not live in him? Consequently in all our dealings with other men we must realize ourselves to be often, if not always, facing the questions that were asked of Cain and Judas.

If we are disciples of Christ we are necessarily our brother's keepers. And the question that is being asked of us concerns all men. It concerns, at the present moment, the entire human race.

We cannot ignore this question. We cannot give an irresponsible and unchristian consent to the demonic use of power for the destruction of a whole nation, a whole continent, or possibly even the whole human race. Or can we? The question is now being asked.

This is the question that forms the subject of the present essay.

In this most critical moment of history we have a twofold task. It is a task in which the whole race is to some degree involved. But the greatest responsibility of all rests upon the citizens of the great power blocs which hold the fate of other nations in their hands.

On one hand we have to defend and foster the highest human values: the right of man to live freely and develop his life in a way worthy of his moral greatness. On the other hand we have to protect man against the criminal abuse of the enormous destructive power which he has acquired. To the American and Western European, this twofold task seems reducible in practice to a struggle against totalitarian dictatorship and against war.

Our very first obligation is to interpret the situation accurately, and this means resisting the temptation to oversimplify and generalize. The struggle against totalitarianism is directed not only against an external enemy—Communism, but also against our own hidden tendencies towards fascist or totalist aberrations. The struggle against war is directed not only against the bellicosity of the Communist powers, but against our own violence, fanaticism and greed. Of course, this kind of thinking will not be popular in the tensions of the cold war. No one is encouraged to be too clearsighted, because conscience can make cowards, by diluting the strong conviction that our side is fully right and the other side is fully wrong. Yet the Christian responsibility is not to one side or to the other in the power struggle: it is to God and truth, and to the whole of mankind.

This is not a political study. But the moral options of our times are necessarily involved in various interpretations of political reality. The different views of the situation prevailing in the West react upon each other, and all together they combine to create extreme difficulties and complexities. The question arises then whether man is really capable of choosing peace rather than nuclear war, whether the choices are ineluctably made for him by the interplay of social forces. The answer to this question must depend on many factors beyond the control of any individual or any one group. But the fact remains that we cannot face the moral issue as free and rational beings unless we can still assume that our freedom and rationality have a meaning. If we are not able to choose to survive, then all discussion of the present crisis is pointless. If we are still free, then this essay can be considered as a very imperfect contribution to the work of moral renewal which is absolutely necessary if we are to make significant use of our freedom.

Freedom does not operate in a void. It is guided, or should be guided, by the light of intelligence. It should conform to a rational estimate of reality. It should not be simply an arbitrary exercise of choice. Blind affirmation of will is irrational and tends to destroy freedom. In any case, however, whether rational or not, freedom depends necessarily on man's concept of himself and of the situation in which he finds himself. If he is able to grasp clearly and realistically the truth of his plight, even though that plight may be desperate or extremely perilous, he can make good use of his freedom and can transcend even the most tragic injustices and be more truly a man because of them. He can turn defeat into victory. On the other hand, the will that is obsessed with power can refuse to see and to assess vitally important realities. It can remain obdurate and closed in the presence of human facts that contradict its obsessions. It is often precisely the will to power that is most stubborn in refusing to accept evidence of goodness and of hope. The blind drive to self-assertion rejects indications that love might be more meaningful and more powerful than force.

One of our most important tasks today is to clear the atmosphere so that men can understand their plight without hatred, without fury, without desperation, and with the minimum of good will. A humble and objective seriousness is necessary for the long task of restoring mutual confidence and preparing the way for the necessary work of collaboration in building world peace. This restoration of a climate of relative sanity is perhaps more important than specific decisions regarding the morality of this or that strategy, this or that pragmatic policy.

And so this essay will concern itself with the climate of opinion and thought in the years of crisis in which we live. Public opinion is intimately concerned with the decisions of authority, decisions which may affect the life and death of millions of people. It is therefore in the general climate of thought (or of thoughtlessness) that moral and sociological epidemics—of panic, hatred, destruction—take their origin. There are certain "climates" of opinion which make it practically impossible to solve civil or international problems except by resort to violence. When such a climate exists, certainly the fact ought to be recognized and something ought to be done about it. And that explains Pope John's encyclical *Pacem in Terris*. In a document devoted to the question of war and peace in the nuclear age, relatively little is said about war itself. The greater part of the encyclical concentrates on basic principles: the dignity of the human person and the primacy of the universal common good over the particular good of the political unit. Above all, Pope John realized that his main job was one of "clearing the air" morally, psychologically and spiritually. To a world lost in a pea-soup fog of exhausting and half comprehended technicalities about law, economics, politics, weaponry, technology etc., the Pope did not offer a series of casuistic solutions to complex and detailed questions. He recalled the minds of men to the fundamental ideas on which peace among nations and races must always depend. In other words, he tried to recreate for them the climate of thought in which they could *see* their objectives in a human and even a hopeful light, and he invited them at least for a moment to emerge from the obscurity and smog of arguments that are without issue. The world was grateful for this moment of fresh air, and in political life, especially on the international level, the smallest gestures and advances toward peace should be accepted with gratitude. Many such gestures followed the publication of *Pacem in Terris* on Holy Thursday of 1963. So many in fact that there has been a significant relaxation of tensions, at least between the U.S. and the USSR.

Without flattering ourselves that we are on the way to a quick solution of our problems, or even that the world at large has fully committed itself to implementing Pope John's Encyclical of Peace, we can at least recognize that such things are possible. We are not utterly condemned to think our way into an impasse from which the only issue is destructive violence. Human and reasonable solutions are still open to us. But they depend on our climate of thought, that is to say, on our ability to hope in peaceful solutions.

A weather map is necessarily very superficial. The storm areas in thought and opinion are not all concentrated on one side or the other of the iron curtain. On both sides extremists, characterized by negativism, distrust of the other side, suspicion, fear, hate and the willingness to resort to force, are very outspoken and have access to the mass media so that their opinions often take on the appearance of quasi-dogmatic finality and are uncritically accepted, with a few unspoken reservations, perhaps, by the majority of the population. Not that most men want war, or even willingly face the possibility that certain trends might lead suddenly to war, but they assume, in a guarded and more or less resigned silence, that the most menacing voices are probably right and that what is printed in most of the papers and shouted from most of the house-tops must quite probably represent a more or less coherent interpretation of political reality. They know that total war is always possible, yet they blindly and confusedly hope that what they refuse to think about is so "unthinkable" that it will never occur, and so they busy themselves with the absorbing rush of life and unconsciously withdraw from any kind of dissenting commitment that would leave them exposed to ostracism. They submit and conform, and trust to the protective coloring that conformity provides in a mass society.

The current moral climate is one of more or less resigned compliance with the world-view popularized by the mass media.

Apart from a very small minority who demand uncompromising unilateral initiatives toward peace, the necessity of force and military strength seems unquestionable to the majority. But there are of course considerable differences of attitude, and many gradations in the opinions of statesmen, strategists and dictators of opinion. Indeed, reflection on strategy in the nuclear age has at times assumed the appearance of an esoteric cult to which only the expert with access to a computer can really consider himself initiated. There is unquestionably a sincere desire for peace, or at least an earnest desire to avoid total war, in the minds of most policy-makers. But the legacy of recent history and the frustrating ambiguities of the international situation seem to make really effective steps toward peace impossible. In the minds of the world leaders a continued stalemate is accepted, in practice, as "peace," and the power struggle continues under the constant menace of accidental global war.

Therefore, though there are many good minds earnestly concerned with the technical problem of peace, and many plans have been proposed and even initiated, the details of this peace-thinking do not reach and illuminate the mind of the common man. For him there remains only the confused apprehension of a perilous situation in which force or the threat of force is a practical necessity, war a proximate danger, and peace at best a fond hope.

Pope John reflects on this climate of confusion and practical despair. "How strongly does the turmoil of individual men and peoples contrast with the perfect order of the universe! *It is as if the relationships which bind them together could only be controlled by force!*" (*Pacem in Terris*, n.4) And he adds: "*The fickleness of opinion often produces this error, that many think that the relationships between men and states can be governed by the same laws as the forces and irrational elements of the universe.*" (n.6)

While praising and fully accepting science, Pope John protests against the common opinion which deifies pseudo-science and leaves man's freedom subject to a vague determinism of laws and forces, thus failing to see that man's freedom and intelligence are the instruments by which he elevates himself above his material surroundings and controls his own destiny by living according to truth, justice and love.

Pope John's message of freedom calls man, first of all, to liberate himself from the climate of confusion and desperation in which he finds himself because he passively accepts and follows a mindless determinism.

Though there are significant differences in ideology in the different power blocs, nevertheless the stratification of opinion is more or less the same everywhere. The extremists on both sides are mirror images of each other.

The thought that is obsessed with war puts aside other considerations and concentrates on the fact that one is threatened with attack, indeed with destruction. This type of thinker is convinced that only the strongest measures are of any use. He distrusts negotiation because he is sure that the adversary is an arch deceiver, and because he is so sure of this he thinks that he himself has to resort to deception whenever possible, so as not to be deceived. He is convinced that the enemy will attack him violently as soon as he thinks he can get away with it. In this climate of thought, strategy tends to work around to the idea of "hitting the enemy before he hits me first."

The crude simplicity of this view tends to recommend it to the average man who does not have time to do a great deal of thinking and who, in any case, does not have access to the more selective and thoughtful sources of information which might enable him to form a more sophisticated judgement. It is clear, and its sweeping ruthlessness gives it an appearance of realism. But unfortunately it maintains a moral and political atmosphere of fear and hatred in which it is more difficult even for "experts" to view things with objective detachment. Who is to say to what extent the statesmen themselves are influenced, in practice, by the horrendous mythology of the mass man? The leaders help to make a myth by their own pronouncements and slogans, and because the myth is so willingly believed by the common man they themselves assume that this is a kind of divine ratification. *Vox populi vox Dei.*

That there are large numbers of Christians who live somewhat easily in this climate of opinion is clear from the popular religious press. This is not surprising if we reflect that most Christians belong to the rank and file of common humanity and that the Catholic press has a tendency to follow accepted and prevalent opinions in matters of world politics. It is also possible that a certain negativism and pessimism which has been widespread in both Catholic and Protestant spirituality since the Renaissance and the Reformation may account for the willingness with which believers accept the idea of a crusade against nations that can quite easily be caricatured as essentially wicked and perverse: made up of beings hardly human, never deserving of trust, always worthy of being destroyed.

This was what prompted Pope John to speak out against the abuse of the mass media, both in *Mater et Magistra* and *Pacem in Terris*. A falsely informed public with a distorted view of political reality and an oversimplified, negative attitude toward other races and peoples, cannot be expected to react in any other way than with irrational and violent responses. Therefore the Pope condemned the dissemination of prejudice and hate by the mass media and said: "Truth demands that the various media of social communication . . . be used with serene objectivity . . . Methods of information which fall short of the truth and by that very token impair the reputation of this or that people, must be discarded." (*Pacem in Terris*, n.90)

An important element in *Pacem in Terris* is Pope John's repeated insistence that one of the basic rights of free man is "the right to be informed truthfully about public events" (n.12), along with the right both to basic and higher education (n.13), the right to form associations to defend their just aims (n.s 23,24), and to take an active (not passive) part in public affairs (n.25). One who merely echoes the opinions in the newspaper is not taking an "active" part in the life of his nation. Hence Pope John's paragraphs on human rights imply not only the privilege but also at times the obligation of dissent from a prevailing and passively accepted viewpoint. And this is extremely important when we consider the context of war and peace, since in a time of crisis and mass-emotionalism the dissenter who maintains his insistence on the rights of peace is easily regarded as a traitor. Nevertheless such dissent may acquire a decisive importance, and it should always be protected by law against arbitrary attack and suppression (n.27). Rights also imply obligations, and the "right to investigate the truth freely (is correlative with) the duty of seeking it ever more completely and profoundly" (n.29). It is unfortunate that the advantages of freedom in a democratic society have been so little appreciated and that men have abdicated their right and neglected their opportunity in order to remain passive, confused and hopeless, not using the sources of information and dissenting opinions to which they might have access.

Cardinal Suenens speaking to the United Nations on May 13, 1963 and explaining the encyclical *Pacem in Terris,* compared it to a symphony with the leitmotif: "Peace among all peoples requires: Truth as its foundation, justice as its rule, love as its driving force, liberty as its atmosphere."

But in the moral climate of mass opinion, engineered by publicists, "truth" tends to mean a sensational revelation of some new iniquity on the part of the enemy. And the misfortune is that on both sides there is enough real iniquity around to make the concoction of sensational news items quite easy. Justice, in this climate, operates on a double standard: one for one's own side and another for the enemy, so that what in him is criminal is, in us, simple "realism." Love is assuredly not the driving force of peace policies which are inert and firmly rooted in inveterate distrust. Liberty is not exactly the mark of relationships in which big powers reduce smaller ones to the status of political or economic satellites. Yet, says Cardinal Suenens, these four are "the rules of the road which lead to peace, rules which must be respected in the relations between various political communities."

Perhaps the chief reason why these rules are neglected are that the most basic principles of human social life are not respected. *Pacem in Terris* reminds us that mankind is one family in which all nations, groups and individuals must cooperate, on the basis of truth, justice, love and liberty in attaining the universal common good which is also at the same time the good of the individual person in his individuality, in his dignity and in his basic rights. If man does not seek, by reasonable collaboration, to attain these ends, there is no alternative but the arbitrary exercise of the will to power, in which case the law of reason, of nature and of God is usurped by the law of the jungle. A theologian commenting on *Pacem in Terris* says:

If owing to antiphilosophic prejudice, universal truths dictated by reason are rejected and only the manifestations of the changing will of nations are revered, whatever these may be, it would be absurd to attempt the construction of a juridical organization of the human race.

(P. Riga, "Peace on Earth," p. 33)

The climate of irrationality, confusion and violence which is characteristic of such times as ours is after all nothing new. The circumstances are different, but in the end we can find in our world much that is analogous to the classic description of Athens after the Peloponnesian War. Thucydides masterfully outlines the political situation of a rich society that is in a crisis of decline and change:

War destroys the comfortable routine of life, trains us in violence and shapes our character according to the new conditions . . . The cause of all these evils was imperialism, whose fundamental motives are ambition and greed, and from which arises the fanaticism of class conflict. The politicians on each side were armed with high sounding slogans . . . Both boasted that they were servants of the community and both made the community the prize of war. The only purpose of their policy was the extermination of their opponents, and to achieve this they stopped at nothing. Even worse were the reprisals which they perpetuated in total disregard of morality or of the common good. The only standard which they recognized was party caprice and so they were prepared, either by the perversion of justice or by revolutionary action, to satisfy the passing passions begotten by the struggle . . . Society was divided into warring camps suspicious of one another. Where no contract or obligation was binding, nothing could heal the conflict, and since security was only to be found in the assumption that nothing was secure, everyone took steps to preserve himself and no one could afford to trust his neighbor. On the whole the baser types survived best. Aware of their own deficiencies and their opponents' abilities, they resorted boldly to violence, before they were defeated in debate, and struck down, by conspiracy, minds more versatile than their own.

(Thucydides, *Peloponnesian War*, iii, 82)

In such a situation, Plato, who hoped that a return to reason could be brought about by the participation of the philosopher in public life, also recognized that intelligent men would be tempted to withdraw from a situation they regarded as "hopeless." The lover of justice, Plato wrote, seeing himself as though thrown into a "den of beasts" and unable to change the jungle law around him;

Will remain quietly at his own work like a traveller caught in a storm who retreats behind a wall to shelter from the driving gusts of dust and hail. Seeing the rest of the world full of iniquity, he will be content to keep his own life on earth untainted by wickedness and impious actions, so that he may leave this world with a fair hope of the next, at peace with himself and God.

(*Republic,* 496)

It is perhaps true that sometimes individuals may be forced into this position, but to view it as normal and to accept it as preferable to the risks and conflicts of public life is an admission of defeat, an abdication of responsibility. This secession into individualistic concern with one's own salvation alone may in fact leave the way all the more open for unscrupulous men and groups to gain and wield unjust power.

The example of Taoism in China in the chaotic period of the 3rd to the 1st centuries B.C. is there to show how an other-worldly spiritualism in public life can end in the worst kind of arbitrary tyranny. The intellectual and the spiritual man cannot therefore justify themselves in abandoning society to the rule of an irrational will to power.

If sheer arbitrary will and brute force are not to take command of everything, reason must seek more solid and more harmonious solutions to problems by arbitration and discussion. Men must collaborate sincerely in solving their difficulties. This is a basic Christian obligation.

But rational collaboration is manifestly impossible without mutual trust and this in turn is out of the question where there is no basis for sure communication. Not only is communication lacking: it is blocked. It is fiercely resisted by groups and nations which close themselves in upon themselves and refuse to communicate with one another except by ultimatums and threats of destruction. Not only that, but esoteric thought systems and complex vocabularies erect barriers that only a specialist can penetrate. Thus the failure of communication between the great powers leads to resentment, distrust and disillusionment among the others.

A pervasive climate of boredom, exasperation and indifference tends to prevail where the grosser moods of bellicism and fanaticism are seen for what they are. A reviewer in *Commentary* summarizing the argument of a book on this subject, gives us in a readable paragraph the picture of

liberal and neo-conservative discontent in Europe
and the "emerging nations."

The cold war from being a necessary defensive operation against the armed threat emanating from the
USSR in 1948 has turned into an endless struggle for
global hegemony: a struggle that neither side can (and
perhaps no longer wants to) win. Meanwhile the neu-
trals are getting restive: Asia, Africa and Latin America
want to break out of this straitjacket. Industrialization
—whether capitalist or socialist—has become *the* pre-
occupation of elites who speak for two-thirds of mankind: the hungry two-thirds. Yet all the while Washington and Moscow exchange verbal brickbats amidst
growing boredom and indifference, and latterly to the
accompaniment of catcalls from Peking . . .

("The Cold War in Perspective," by George Lichtheim,
Commentary, June 1964, p. 25.)

So, while the policies of force continue to in-
voke traditional notions of justice, rights, international law, etc., the repetition of these formulas
makes them sound more and more hollow and absurd to everyone. This climate of disillusionment
and disgust is dangerous because it implies a growing contempt for reason and for the basic human
powers without which man cannot organize his
life in a free and orderly fashion. This engenders
a deeper pessimism, a more tenacious hopelessness,
and communication becomes more and more pre-
carious.

Pacem in Terris certainly recognized that Catholics themselves were to a great extent out of contact with the rest of the world, enclosed in their own spiritual and religious ghetto. One of the chief contributions of Pope John's brief pontificate was that he opened the ghetto and told Catholics to go out and talk to other people, to Protestants, to Jews, to Hindus, and even to Communists. He realized that without this climate of openness, the communication which was essential for mutual trust would be out of the question. He insisted on making a "clear distinction between false philosophical teachings . . . and movements which have a direct bearing either on economic or social questions or cultural matters . . ." (*Pacem in Terris,* n.159) It is necessary to communicate with those who hold different ideologies when we are confronting common problems that can only be solved in collaboration. If we speak different languages we must nevertheless attempt to find the essential points of agreement without which there is, as Cardinal Suenens says, a permanent risk of disaster. We must therefore either decide to continue in a fatal rivalry or begin to trust one another in progressive negotiations in which peace may eventually be stabilized and guaranteed.

It is the attitude of openness prescribed by *Pacem in Terris* that must form our thinking as Christians in time of crisis, and not the closed and fanatical myths of nationalistic or racial paranoia. Only if we remain open, detached, humble in the presence of objective truth and of our fellow man, will we be able to choose peace.

2. THE CHRISTIAN AS PEACEMAKER

Like his predecessor in the papacy, like all deeply religious and indeed all truly rational men, Pope John XXIII deplored the gigantic stockpiles of weapons, the arms race and the cold war. He asked the leaders of the great powers to bring the arms race to an end and come "to an agreement on a fitting program of disarmament, employing mutual and effective controls" (*Pacem in Terris,* n.122). This and other passages of the Peace Encyclical, where Pope John speaks of disarmament and modern warfare, have often been quoted and need not be repeated here. But it is more important to observe that Pope John did not merely call for the reduction of weapons and the easing of international tensions. He asserted that there was really no hope of this being done effectively unless it was prompted by deep inner conviction. Such conviction demands that "everyone sincerely cooperates to banish the fear and anxious expectation of war with which men are oppressed."

Once again we see that Pope John was chiefly concerned with the general climate of thought and the current moral outlook of mankind. It would be of little use for one side or the other, or both, to disarm, if men continued in the same state of confusion, suspicion, hostility and aggressiveness.

Therefore, if a climate favorable to peace is to be produced, Pope John continues, "the fundamental principle upon which our present peace depends must be replaced by another, which declares that the true and solid peace of nations consists not in equality of arms but in mutual trust alone. We believe that this can be brought to pass, and we consider that, since it concerns a matter not only demanded by right reason but also eminently desirable in itself, it will prove the source of many benefits." (n. 113)

But it would be sentimental to ask men to awaken feelings of optimism and trust in their hearts without laying that firm foundation of order which *Pacem in Terris* repeatedly demands as the essential condition for true peace on earth.

"Peace will be an empty sounding word unless it is founded on the order which this present document has outlined in confident hope: an order founded on truth, built according to justice, vivified and integrated by charity, and put into practice in freedom." (n.168) The duty of working together for peace in this sense binds not only public authority but all those to whom the Encyclical is addressed: that is to say *everybody*. But of course it is a special obligation of the Christian who, as a follower of Christ, must be a peacemaker.

Pope John understood and clearly stated that being a "peacemaker" meant more, not less, than being a "pacifist." It is not only a matter of protesting against the bomb, but also of working tirelessly and constructively at the "most exalted task of bringing about true peace in the order established by God . . . (by establishing) *new methods of relationships in human society*." (n.163) Pope John publicly and emphatically praises the few who have devoted themselves to this work, and hopes "that their number will increase, especially among those who believe." (n. 164)

Let us reflect on the emphasis with which Pope John called Christians, in the name of Christ their Head, to this work of peace based on truth, justice, love and liberty in human relations. This summons to fight in the ranks of an army of peace is of course traditionally Christian, and yet it is also new because it occurs in a context so new that Cardinal Suenens called it "unprecedented in history."

Pope John's call to peace was based not on distrust of man and denunciation of his wickedness, but on the assertion of man's fundamental goodness. Not only the material world, not only technological society, but even the society built by unbelievers and enemies of the Church with the aim of raising man to a better temporal state, is regarded by Pope John with eyes of friendly concern. Not only does he tolerate the presence of a non-Christian society, but he embraces it in the love of Christ. The context of Christian peacemaking is then something other than that even of so-called Christian pacifism. This must be brought out, because there are certain ambiguities in the term "pacifist" which lay it open to manipulation and misinterpretation by those for whom world peace is not a seriously credible option, except on a basis of overwhelming force.

No need to mention the facile caricature of the "pacifist" as a maladjusted creature lost in impractical ideals, sentimentally hoping that prayer and demonstrations can convert men to the ways of peace. It is routine for the mass media to treat even the most eminent and reasonable defenders of peace, men with a worldwide reputation as scientists, as if they were slightly addled egg-heads as well as communist sympathizers, or indeed undercover agents of Moscow. I refer rather to fundamental religious ambiguities in the term "pacifism." Actually it is often hard to pin these ambiguities down with precision. They depend in each case on the implicit spiritual bases of the pacifism in question, and these are not easy to find.

Often "pacifism" in the religious sense is rooted in a world-denying and individualistic asceticism, or it is found in the context of a small eschatalogical community (like that of the Shakers for instance) which also may have other beliefs, rejecting marriage, the use of flesh meat, etc., which in their turn may be justified by a kind of manichaean theology. In other words a pacifism that regards war as an inevitable and intolerable evil, as intolerable as the unregenerate world from which it cannot be separated, and which the individual believer must renounce, by that very fact tends to rejoin the pessimism of the belligerent crusader who implicitly carries his denial of the world to the point of wishing it to be destroyed.

Probably no one has ever accused *Pacem in Terris* of being "pacifist," and there is good reason not to do so. There is in this document nothing of the world-hating rejection that identifies war with the city of man. Pope John's optimism was really something new in Christian thought because he expressed the unequivocal hope that a world of ordinary men, a world in which many men were not Christians or even believers in God, might still be a world of peace if men would deal with one another on the basis of their God-given reason and with respect for their inalienable human rights. Note that *Pacem in Terris* is the first encyclical in which the language of human rights has been so clearly espoused.

The religious ambiguities in the term "pacifism" give it implications that are somewhat less than Catholic. I do not here refer to the inaccurate and perverse generalization that "a Catholic cannot be a conscientious objector," but to the fact that "pacifism" tends, as a cause, to take on the air of a quasi-religion, as though it were a kind of faith in its own right. A pacifist is then regarded as one who "believes in peace" so to speak as an article of faith, and hence puts himself in the position of being absolutely unable to countenance any form of war, since for him to accept any war in theory or in practice would be to deny his faith. A Christian pacifist then becomes one who compounds this ambiguity by insisting, or at least by implying, that pacifism is an integral part of Christianity, with the evident conclusion that Christians who are not pacifists have, by that fact, apostatized from Christianity.

This unfortunate emphasis gains support from the way conscientious objection is in fact treated by the selective service laws of the United States. An objector who is a religious "pacifist" is considered as one who for subjective and personal reasons of conscience and belief refuses to go to war, and whose "conscientious objection" is tolerated and even recognized by the government. There is of course something valuable and edifying in this recognition of the personal conscience, but there is also an implication that any minority stand against war on grounds of conscience is ipso facto a kind of deviant and morally eccentric position, to be tolerated only because there are always a few religious half-wits around in any case, and one has to humor them in order to preserve the nation's reputation for respecting individual liberty.

In other words, this sanctions the popular myth that all pacifism is based on religious emotion rather than on reason, and that it has no objective ethical validity, but is allowed to exist because of the possibility of harmless and mystical obsessions with peace on the part of a few enthusiasts. It also sanctions another myth, to which some forms of pacifism give support, that pacifists are people who simply prefer to yield to violence and evil rather than resist it in any way. They are fundamentally indifferent to reasonable, moral or patriotic ideals and prefer to sink into their religious apathy and let the enemy overrun the country unresisted.

To sum it all up in a word, this caricature of pacifism which reduces it to a purely eccentric individualism of conscience, declares that the pacifist is willing to let everyone be destroyed merely because he himself does not have a taste for war. It is not hard to imagine what capital can be made out of this distortion by copy writers for, say, *Time* magazine or the New York *Daily News*. It is also easy to see how the Catholic clergy might be profoundly suspicious of any kind of conscientious objection to war when myths like these have helped them to form their judgement.

Speaking in the name of Christ and of the Church to all mankind, Pope John was not issuing a pacifist document in this sense. He was not simply saying that if a few cranks did not like the bomb they were free to entertain their opinion. He was saying, on the contrary, that we had reached a point in history where it was clearly no longer reasonable to make use of war in the settlement of international disputes, and that the important thing was not merely protest against the latest war technology, but the construction of permanent world peace on a basis of truth, justice, love and liberty. This is not a matter for a few individual consciences, it urgently binds the conscience of every living man. It is not an individual refinement of spirituality, a luxury of the soul, but a collective obligation of the highest urgency, a universal and immediate need which can no longer be ignored.

He is not saying that a few Christians may and

ought to be pacifists (i.e., to protest against war)
but that all Christians and all reasonable men are
bound by their very rationality to work to establish a real and lasting peace.

Already in his first encyclical, *Ad Petri Cathe-
dram*, Pope John had said that Christians were
obliged to strive "with all the means at their disposal" for peace. Yet he warned that peace cannot
compromise with error or make concessions to injustice. Passive acquiescence in injustice, submission to brute force are not the way to genuine
peace. There is some truth in Machiavelli's contention that mere weakness and confusion lead in the
long run to greater disasters than a firm and even
intransigent policy. But the Christian program for
peace does not depend on human astuteness, ruthlessness or force. Power can never be the keystone
of a Christian policy. Yet our work for peace must
be energetic, enlightened and fully purposeful. Its
purpose is defined by our religious belief that God
has called us "to the service of His merciful de-
signs" (John XXIII, Christmas Message, 1958).
If we are now in possession of atomic power, we
have the moral obligation to make a good and
peaceful use of it, rather than turning it to our
own destruction. But we will not be able to do this
without an interior revolution that abandons the
quest for brute power and submits to the wisdom
of love and of the Cross.

It must however be stated quite clearly and without compromise that the duty of the Christian as a peacemaker is not to be confused with a kind of quietistic inertia that is indifferent to injustice, accepts any kind of disorder, compromises with error and with evil, and gives in to every pressure in order to maintain "peace at any price." The Christian knows well, or should know well, that peace is not possible on such terms. Peace demands the most heroic labor and the most difficult sacrifice. It demands greater heroism than war. It demands greater fidelity to the truth and a much more perfect purity of conscience. The Christian fight for peace is not to be confused with defeatism.

What is the traditional attitude of the Christian peacemaker? Let us glance back over a few sources and briefly examine some traditional witnesses to the Christian concern for peace on earth.

Christians believe that Christ came into this world as a Prince of Peace. We believe that Christ Himself is our peace (Eph. 2:14). We believe that God has chosen for Himself, in the Mystical Body of Christ, an elect people, regenerated by the Blood of the Savior, and committed by their baptismal promise to wage war upon the evil and hatred that are in man, and help to establish the Kingdom of God and of peace, in truth and love.

Indeed for centuries the Old Testament pro-

phets had been looking forward to the coming of
the Messias as the "Prince of Peace" (Isaias 9:6).
The Messianic Kingdom was to be a kingdom of
peace because first of all man would be completely
reconciled with God and with the hostile forces of
nature (Osee 2:18–20) the whole world would
be full of the manifest knowledge of the divine
mercy (Isaias 11:9) and hence men, the sons of
God and objects of His mercy, would live at peace
with one another (Isaias 54:13). The early Christians were filled with the conviction that since the
Risen Christ had received Lordship over the whole
cosmos and sent His Spirit to dwell in men (Acts
2:17) the kingdom of peace was already established in the Church.

This meant a recognition that human nature,
identical in all men, was assumed by the Logos in
the Incarnation, and that Christ died out of love
for all men, in order to live in all men. All were
henceforth "one in Christ" (Gal. 3:28) and
Christ Himself was their peace, since His Spirit
kept them united in supernatural love (Eph. 4:3).
The Christian therefore has the obligation to treat
every other man as Christ Himself, respecting his
neighbor's life as if it were the life of Christ, his
rights as if they were the rights of Christ. Even
if that neighbor shows himself to be unjust,
wicked and odious to us, the Christian cannot take
upon himself a final and definitive judgement in

his case. The Christian still has an obligation to be patient, and to seek his enemy's highest spiritual interests and indeed his temporal good in so far as that may be compatible with the universal common good of man.

The Christian commandment to love our enemies was not regarded by the first Christians merely as a summons to higher moral perfection than was possible under the Old Law. The New Law did not compete with the Old, but on the contrary fulfilled it, at the same time abolishing the conflicts between various forms of obligation and perfection. The love of enemies was not therefore the expression of a Christian moral ideal, in contrast with Stoic, Epicurean or Jewish ideals. It was much more an expression of eschatalogical faith in the realization of the messianic promises and hence a witness to an entirely new dimension in man's life.

Christian peace was therefore not considered at first to be simply a religious and spiritual consecration of the Pax Romana. It was an eschatalogical gift of the Risen Christ. (John 20:19) It could not be achieved by any ethical or political program. It was given with the supreme gift of the Holy Spirit, making men spiritual and uniting them to the "mystical" Body of Christ. Christian peace is in fact a fruit of the Spirit (Galatians 5:22) and a sign of the Divine Presence in the world.

Division, conflict, strife, schism, hatreds and wars are then evidence of the "old life," the unregenerate sinful existence that has not been transformed in the mystery of Christ (I Cor. 1:10; James 3:16). When Christ told Peter to "put away his sword" (John 18:11) and warned him that those who struck with the sword would perish by it, He was not simply forbidding war. War was neither blessed nor forbidden by Christ. He simply stated that war belonged to the world outside the Kingdom, the world outside the mystery and the Spirit of Christ and that therefore for one who was seriously living in Christ, war belonged to a realm that no longer had a decisive meaning, for though the Christian was "in the world" he was not "of the world." He could not avoid implication in its concerns, but he belonged to a kingdom of peace "that was not of this world" (John 18:36).

The Christian is and must be by his very adoption as a son of God, In Christ, a peacemaker (Matt. 5:9). He is bound to imitate the Savior who, instead of defending Himself with twelve legions of angels (Matt. 26:55), allowed Himself to be nailed to the Cross and died praying for His executioners. The Christian is one whose life has sprung from a particular spiritual seed: the blood of the martyrs who, without offering forcible resistance, laid down their lives rather than submit to the unjust laws that demanded an official religious cult of the Emperor as God. One verse in St. John's account of the Passion of Christ makes clear the underlying principles of war and peace in the Gospel (John 18:36). Questioned by Pilate as to whether He is a King, Jesus replies "My Kingdom is not of this world" and explains that if he were a worldly king his followers would be fighting for him. In other words, the Christian attitude to war and peace is fundamentally eschatalogical. The Christian does not need to fight and indeed it is better that he should not fight, for in so far as he imitates his Lord and Master, he proclaims that the Messianic kingdom has come and bears witness to the presence of the *Kyrios Pantocrator* in mystery, even in the midst of the conflicts and turmoil of the world. The book of the New Testament that definitely canonizes this eschatalogical view of peace in the midst of spiritual combat is the Apocalypse, which sets forth in mysterious and symbolic language the critical struggle of the nascent Church with the powers of the world, as typified by the Roman Empire.

This struggle, which is definitive and marks the last age of the world, is the final preparation for the manifestation of Christ as Lord of the Universe (the *Parousia*) (Apocalypse 11:15–18). The Kingdom is already present in the world, since Christ has overcome the world and risen from the dead. But the Kingdom is still not fully manifested and remains outwardly powerless. It is a kingdom of saints and martyrs, priests and witnesses, whose main function is to bide their time in faith, loving one another and the truth, suffering persecution in the furious cataclysm which marks the final testing of earthly society. They will take no direct part in the struggles of earthly kingdoms. Their life is one of faith, gentleness, meekness, patience, purity. They depend on no power other than the power of God, and it is God they obey rather than the state, which tends to usurp the powers of God and to blaspheme Him, setting itself up in His stead as an idol and drawing to itself the adoration and worship that are due to Him alone (Apoc. 13:3–9).

The Apocalypse describes the final stage of the history of the world as a total and ruthless power struggle in which all the Kings of the earth are engaged, but which has an inner, spiritual dimension these kings are incapable of seeing and understanding. The wars, cataclysms and plagues which convulse worldly society are in reality the outward projection and manifestation of a hidden, spiritual battle. Two dimensions, spiritual and material, cut across one another. To be consciously and willingly committed to the worldly power struggle, in politics, business and war, is to founder in darkness, confusion, and sin. The saints are "in the world" and doubtless suffer from its murderous conflicts like everybody else. Indeed they seem at first to be defeated and destroyed (13:7). But they see the inner meaning of these struggles and are patient. They trust in God to work out their destiny and rescue them from the final destruction, the accidents of which are not subject to their control. Hence they pay no attention to the details of the power struggle as such and do not try to influence it or to engage in it, one way or another, even for their own apparent benefit and survival. For they realize that their survival has nothing to do with the exercise of force or ingenuity.

The ever recurrent theme of the Apocalypse is then that the typical power-structured empire of Babylon (Rome) cannot but be "drunk with the blood of the martyrs of Jesus" (17:6) and that therefore the saints must "go out from her" and break off all relations with her and her sinful concerns (18:4 ff) for "in one hour" is her judgement decided and the smoke of the disaster "shall go up forever and ever" (19:3). Yet the author of the Apocalypse does not counsel flight, as there is no geographical escape from Babylon: the one escape is into a spiritual realm by martyrdom, to lay down one's life in fidelity to God and in protest against the impurity, the magic, the fictitiousness and the murderous fury of the city whose god is force (21:4–8).

What is the place of war in all this? War is the "rider of the red horse" who is sent to prepare the destruction of the power-structure (6:4) for "he has received power to take away peace from the earth and to make them all kill one another, and he has received a great sword." The four horsemen (war, hunger, death and pestilence) are sent as signs and precursors of the final consummation of history. Those who have led the saints captive will themselves be made captive, those who have killed the saints will themselves be killed in war: and the saints in their time will be rescued from the cataclysm by their patience (13:10).

Translated into historical terms, these mysterious symbols of the Apocalypse show us the early Christian attitude toward war, injustice and the persecutions of the Roman empire, even though that empire was clearly understood to possess a demonic power. The battle was non-violent and spiritual, and its success depended on the clear understanding of the totally new and unexpected dimensions in which it was to be fought. On the other hand, there is no indication whatever in the Apocalypse that the Christian would be willing to fight and die to maintain the "power of the beast," in other words to engage in a power-struggle for the benefit of the Emperor and of his power.

Nevertheless, it must not be stated without qualification that all the early Christians were purely and simply pacifists and that they had a clear, systematic policy of pacifism which obliged them to refuse military service whenever it was demanded of them. This would be too sweeping an assertion. There were Christians in the armies of Rome, but they were doubtless exceptional. Many of them had been converted while they were soldiers and remained in "the state in which they had been called" (I Cor. 7:10). They were free to do so because the Imperial army was considered as a police force, maintaining the *Pax Romana,* and the peace of the empire as Origen said (*Contra Celsum* II, 30) was something the early Church was able to appreciate as in some sense providential. However, the military life was not considered ideal for a Christian. The problem of official idolatry was inescapable. Many Christian soldiers suffered martyrdom for refusing to participate in the sacrifices. Nevertheless, some soldiers, like St Maximilian, were martyred explicitly for refusal to serve in the army. Others, like St Martin of Tours, remained in service until they were called upon to kill in battle, and then refused to do so. Martin, according to the office in the monastic Breviary, declared that "because he was a soldier of Christ it was not licit for him to kill." Christians were the first to lay down their lives rather than fight in war.

The early Christian apologists tend to condemn military service. Clement of Alexandria again takes up the theme of the Christian as a "soldier of peace" whose only weapons are the word of God and the Christian virtues (*Protreptic* XI, 116). Justin Martyr declares in his *Apology* (I, 39), "We who formerly murdered one another (he is a convert from paganism) now not only do not make war upon our enemies, but that we may not lie or deceive our judges, we gladly die confessing Christ." St Cyprian remarked shrewdly that while the killing of one individual by another was recognized as a crime, when homicide is carried out publicly on a large scale by the state it turns into a virtue! (*Ad Donatum,* VI, 10). Tertullian declared that when Christ took away Peter's sword, "he disarmed every soldier" (*De Idololatria,* XIX).

3. WAR IN ORIGEN AND ST AUGUSTINE

It is interesting to examine in some detail the attack on Christianity written by a pagan traditionalist, Celsus, who is refuted in Origen's *Contra*

Celsum. (3rd century A.D.) Celsus is a conservative who is deeply disturbed by the decay of the
Roman Empire, and he agrees with many of his
contemporaries in ascribing that decay to the
nefarious revolutionary influence of the secret
society called Christians. The anxiety which
Celsus, a cultivated pagan, feels over the imminent
downfall of the society to which he belongs, dis-
charges itself in a mixture of contempt and hatred
upon Jews and above all the new sect of Jews who
worship Christ. For though he despises the Jews,
Celsus can tolerate them because their worship
and customs are "at least traditional." But Christianity is completely subversive of the old religious
and social order which Celsus conceives to be
more or less universal and cosmopolitan. His chief
grievance against the Christians is their claim to
exclusiveness, to the possession of a special revealed
truth which forms no part of the socio-religious
heritage of the various nations, but contradicts all
known religions, rejecting them along with the
traditional norms of culture and civilization.
Abandoning the reasonable and universal norms
of polytheism, Christianity, he says, worships a
crucified Jew. Christians are rebels who deliberately cut themselves off from the rest of mankind.
They are undermining the whole fabric of society
with their insidious doctrines. Above all, they are
irresponsible and selfish, indeed anti-social. In-

stead of returning to the customs of their fathers and living content like the rest of men with the *status quo,* they refuse to take part in public life, they do not carry out their duties as citizens, and in particular they *refuse to fight in the army.* In a word, they remain callously indifferent to the service of the threatened empire, and have no concern with peace and order, or with the common good. It is the familiar condemnation of the pacifist: "Just because he perversely refuses to fight, everyone else is threatened with destruction!"

In a word, Celsus reflects the profound insecurity of one who is totally attached to decaying social forms, and who thinks he beholds in some of his contemporaries a complete indifference towards the survival of all that is meaningful to him. Christians, it seemed, not only believed that Celsus' Roman world was meaningless, but that it was under judgement and doomed to destruction. He interpreted the other-worldly Christian spirit as a concrete, immediate physical threat. There was doubtless no other way in which he was capable of understanding it.

Origen replies first of all by vigorously denying that the Christians are violent revolutionaries, or that they have any intention of preparing the overthrow of the empire by force. He says:

Christians have been taught not to defend themselves against their enemies; and because they have kept the laws which command gentleness and love to man, on this account they have received from God that which they would not have succeeded in doing if they had been given the right to make war, even though they may have been quite able to do so. He always fought for them and from time to time stopped the opponents of the Christians and the people who wanted to kill them. (*Contra Celsum*, III, Chadwick, translation, p. 133)

After this Origen takes issue with the basic contention of Celsus that there have to be wars, because men cannot live together in unity. Origen announces the Christian claim that a time will come for all men to be united in the Logos, though this fulfillment is most probably eschatalogical (realized only after the end and fulfillment of world history). Nevertheless, Christians are *not totally unconcerned* with the peace, fortunes and survival of the Empire. Origen does not take the categorically unwordly view of the Apocalypse. He has a great respect for Greek and Roman civilization at least in its more spiritual and humane aspects. The unified Roman world is the providentially appointed scene for the Gospel *kerygma*.

Origen as a matter of fact was far from anti-social, still less anti-intellectual. A man who united in himself profound learning, philosophical culture and Christian holiness, Origen took an urbane, optimistic view of classical thought and of Greco-Roman civilization. Indeed his arguments against Celsus are drawn in large measure from Classical philosophy and demonstrate, by implication, that a Christian was not necessarily an illiterate boor. The chief value of Origen's apologetic lay in his capacity to meet Celsus on the common ground of classical learning.

Notice that Origen and Celsus have radically different notions of society. For Celsus, the social life of men is a complex of accepted traditions and customs which are "given" by the gods of the various nations and have simply to be accepted, for, as Pindar said, "Custom is the king of all." Indeed it is impious to question them or to try to change them. The cults of the gods, the rites and practices associated with those cults, are all good in their own ways, and must be preserved. The Christians who discard all this are plainly subversive and dangerous.

Origen on the other hand sees that human society has been racially transformed by the Incarnation of the Logos. The presence in the world of the Risen Savior, in and through His Church, has destroyed the seeing validity of all that was in reality arbitrary, tyrannical or absurd in the fictions of social life. He has introduced worship and communal life of an entirely new kind, "in spirit and in truth."

The opening lines of the *Contra Celsum* openly declare that it is not only right but obligatory to disobey human laws and ignore human customs when these are contrary to the law of God:

> Suppose that a man were living among the Scythians (cannibals) whose laws are contrary to the Divine law, who had no opportunity to go elsewhere and was compelled to live among them; such a man for the sake of the true law, though illegal among the Scythians, would rightly form associations with like-minded people contrary to the laws of the Scythians . . . It is not wrong to form associations against the errors for the sake of truth.
>
> *(Contra Celsum, 1, 1)*

But among other things, the Christians are united against war, in obedience to Christ. This is one of their chief differences with the rest of society.

> No longer do we take the sword against any nations nor do we learn war any more since we have become the sons of peace through Jesus who is our author instead of following the traditional customs by which we were strangers to the covenant. *(Ibid., V, 33)*

Origen argues, then, that if Christians refuse military service it does not mean that they do not bear their fair share in the common life and responsibilities. They play their part in the life of the *Polis*. But this role is spiritual and transcendent. Christians help the Emperor by their prayers, not by force of arms. "The more pious a man is the more effective he is in helping the emperors—more so than the soldiers who go out into the lines and kill all the enemy troops that they can." (III, 73, Chadwick, p. 509.)

This should not be totally unfamiliar to Celsus. After all pagan priests were officially exempted from military service so that they might be able to offer sacrifices "with hands unstained from blood and pure from murders." Christians both laity and clergy were a "royal priesthood," and did more by their prayers to preserve peace than the army could do by threats of force.

"We who by our prayers destroy all demons which stir up wars, violate oaths and disturb the peace, are of more help to the Emperors than those who seem to be doing the fighting." (*Ibid.,* p. 509).

If at first Origen's claim that the Christians "helped the Emperor" by their prayers may have seemed naive, we see here more clearly what he is driving at. He does not mean that the prayers of the Church enable the Emperor to pursue successfully some policy or other of worldly ambition and power. He does not claim for the prayers of the Church a magic efficacy. He means that prayers are weapons in a more hidden and yet more crucial type of warfare, and one in which the peace of the Empire more truly and certainly depends. In a word, if peace is the objective, spiritual weapons will preserve it more effectively than those which kill the enemy in battle. For the weapon of prayer is not directed against other men, but against the evil forces which divide men into warring camps. If these evil forces are overcome by prayer, then both sides are benefitted, war is avoided and all are united in peace. In other words, the Christian does not help the war effort of one particular nation, but he fights against war itself with spiritual weapons.

This basic principle, that love, or the desire of the good of all men, must underlie all Christian action, reappears even more forcefully in St Augustine. But now we find it incorporated into a defense of the "just war," and the perspective has been completely altered.

Roughly two-hundred years separate the two greatest apologetic works of early Christians against the classical world: Origen's *Contra Celsum* and St Augustine's *City of God*. During these two-hundred years a crucially important change has taken place in the Christian attitude to war. Origen took for granted that the Christian is a peacemaker and does not indulge in warfare. Augustine, on the contrary, pleads with the soldier, Boniface, not to retire to the monastery but to remain in the army and do his duty, defending the North African cities menaced by barbarian hordes.

In these two-hundred years, there have been two events of outstanding importance: the Battle of Milvian bridge in 312, leading to the conversion of Constantine and his official recognition of Christianity and then, in 411, the fall of Rome before the onslaught of Alaric the Goth. When Augustine laid the foundation for Christian theories of the "just war," the barbarians were at the gates of the city of Hippo, where he was bishop.

This is not the place to go into the crucially important question of St Augustine's ideas of the human commonwealth, the earthly City, and its relations with the City of God. Suffice it to say that the question had become far more complex for him than it had ever been for the tranquil and optimistic Origen.

For Augustine, the essence of all society is union in common love for a common end. There are two kinds of love in man—an earthly and selfish love (*amor concupiscentiae*) and a heavenly, spiritual, disinterested love (*caritas*). Hence there are two "cities" based on these two kinds of love. The earthly city of selfish and temporal love for power and gain, and the heavenly city of spiritual charity. It will be seen at once that this distinction throws the followers of Augustine's theology of war in contemporary America into a radically ambivalent position, for the pessimistic Augustinian concept of society directly contradicts the optimistic American ethos. Indeed, the current American concept is that love of earthly and temporal ends is automatically self-regulating and leads to progress and happiness. Our city is frankly built on *concupiscentia*.

Every society, according to Augustine, seeks peace, and if it wages war, it does so for the sake of peace. Peace is the "tranquillity of order." But the notion of order in any given society depends on the love which keeps that society together. The earthly society, in its common pursuit of power and gain, has only an apparent order—it is the order of a band of robbers, cooperating for evil ends. Yet in so far as it is an order at all, it is good. It is better than complete disorder. And yet it is fundamentally a disorder, and the peace of the wicked city is not true peace at all.

Cain is the founder of the earthly city (Genesis 4:17). Abel founded no city at all, but lived on earth as a pilgrim, a member of the only true city, the heavenly Jersualem, the city of true peace. For Augustine, as for the Apocalypse and Origen, all history tends towards the definitive victory of the heavenly city of peace. Yet on earth, citizens of heaven live *among* the citizens of earth, though not *like* them.

This creates a problem. In so far as the Christian lives in the earthly city and participates in its benefits, he is bound to share its responsibilities though they are quite different from those of the heavenly city. Hence he may possess property, he marries and brings up children although in heaven "no one marries or is given in marriage." (Luke 20:34) *And also he participates in the just wars of the earthly city*, unless he is exempted by dedication to a completely spiritual life in the priestly or monastic state.

A pagan, Volusianus, confronted Augustine with the same objection Celsus proposed to Origen. If Christians did not help defend the state, they were anti-social. Augustine replied not that they simply pray for the earthly city, but that they do in all truth participate in is defense by military action, but the war must be a just war and its conduct must be just. In a word, for the earthly city war is sometimes an unavoidable necessity. Christians may participate in the war, or may abstain from participation. But their *motives* will be different from the motives of the pagan soldier. They are not really defending the earthly city, they are waging war to establish peace, since peace is willed by God. So now the attention of the Christian is focused on the interior motive which justifies war: the love of peace to be safeguarded by force.

It is no accident that the Protestant thinkers of our own day who rate as nuclear "realists" and defend war as a practical and unavoidable necessity owe much to Augustine. But this is not a distinction belonging to Protestants alone. All Catholics who defend the just war theory are implicitly following Augustine. *St Augustine is, for better or for worse, the Father of all modern Christian thought on war.*

Can we not say that if there are to be significant new developments in Christian thought on nuclear war, it may well be that these developments will depend on our ability to get free from the overpowering influence of Augustinian assumptions and take a new view of man, of society and of war itself? This may perhaps be attained by a renewed emphasis on the earlier, more mystical and more eschatalogical doctrine if the New Testament and the early Fathers, though not necessarily a return to an imaginary ideal of pure primitive pacifism. It will also require a more optimistic view of man. Certainly Pope John XXIII has done more than anyone else to give us a new perspective.

What are the basic assumptions underlying Augustine's thought on war? First of all, there is one which Celsus the pagan proposed, and Origen rejected: that it is impossible for man to live without getting into violent conflict with other men. Augustine agrees with Celsus. Universal peace in practice is inconceivable. In the early days of the Church this principle might perhaps have been accepted as logical, but then discarded as irrelevant. The eschatalogical perspectives of the early Church were real, literal and immediate. The end was believed to be very near. There would not be time for an indefinite series of future wars.

But Augustine saw the shattered and collapsing Empire attacked on all sides by barbarian armies. War could not be avoided. The question was, then, to find out some way to fight that did not violate the Law of Love. And in order to reconcile war with Christian love, Augustine had recourse to pre-Christian, Classical notions of justice. His ideas on the conduct of the just war were drawn to a considerable extent from Cicero.

How does Augustine justify the use of force, even for a just cause? The external act may be one of violence. War is regrettable indeed. But if one's interior motive is purely directed to a just cause and to love of the enemy, then the use of force is not unjust. This distinction between the external act and the interior intention is entirely characteristic of Augustine. "Love" he says, "does

not exclude wars of mercy waged by the good."
(Letter 138.)

But here we come upon a further, most significant development in Augustine's thought. The
Christian may join the non-Christian in fighting
to preserve peace in the earthly city. But suppose
that the earthly city itself is almost totally made
up of Christians. Then cooperation between the
"two cities" takes on a new aspect, and we arrive
at the conclusion that a "secular arm" of military
force can be called into action against heretics, to
preserve not only civil peace but the purity of faith.
Thus Augustine becomes also the remote fore-
father of the Crusades and of the Inquisition.

"Love does not exclude wars of mercy waged
by the good!" The history of the Middle Ages,
of the Crusades, of the religious wars has taught us
what strange consequences can flow from this
noble principle. Augustine, for all his pessimism
about human nature, did not foresee the logical
results of his thought, and in the original context,
his "wars of mercy" to defend civilized order
make a certain amount of sense. Always his idea
is that the Church and the Christians, whatever
they may do, are aiming at ultimate peace. The
deficiency of Augustinian thought lies therefore
not in the good intentions it prescribes but in an
excessive naiveté with regard to the good that can
be attained by violent means which cannot help

but call forth all that is worst in man. And so, alas, for centuries we have heard kings, princes, bishops, priests, ministers, and the Lord alone knows what variety of unctuous beadles and sacrists, earnestly urging all men to take up arms out of love and mercifully slay their enemies (including other Christians) without omitting to purify their interior intention.

Of course when we read Augustine himself, and when we see that he imposes such limits upon the Christian soldier and traces out such a strict line of conduct for him, we can see that the theory of the just war was not altogether absurd, and that it was capable of working in ages less destructive than our own. But one wonders at the modern Augustinians and at their desperate manoeuvers to preserve the doctrine of the just war from the museum or the junk pile. In the name of "realism" (preserving, that is to say, a suitable dash of Augustinian pessimism about fallen man) they plunge into ambivalence from which Augustine was fortunately preserved by the technological ignorance of his dark age.

Augustine kept a place in his doctrine for a certain vestige of the eschatalogical tradition. There were some Christians who would not be permitted to fight: these were the monks, first of all, the men who had totally left the world and abandoned its concerns to live in the Kingdom of

God, and then the clergy who preached the Gospel of Peace—or at least the Gospel of the merciful war. Yet as Christianity spread over Europe and the ancient Roman strain was vivified and restored by the addition of vigorous barbarian blood from the north, even monks and clerics were sometimes hard to restrain from rushing to arms and loving exuberantly with the sword. Do we not read that when a Frankish ship loaded with Crusaders ran into the Byzantine fleet in the first Crusade, the Byzantines were shocked at a Latin priest who stood on the stern covered with blood and furiously discharged arrows at them, clad in vestments, too: and he even went on shooting after the declaration of a truce.*

Still, there were recognized limits. Councils sternly restricted warfare. In 10th century England a forty-day fast was prescribed as penance for anyone who killed an enemy in war—even in a just war. Killing was regarded as an evil to be atoned for even if it could not be avoided (see Migne, P.L., vol. 79, col. 407). However, later theologians of the Middle Ages (see Migne, P.L., vol. 125, col. 841) made clear that killing in a just war was not a sin and intimated that the soldier who did this required no penance, as

---

* This was in the First Crusade. Quoted from the Alexiad of Anna Comnena, in Bainton, R.H., *Christian Attitudes to War and Peace*, New York and Nashville, 1960, p. 114.

he had done a work pleasing to God. We were then close to the time of the Crusades. But even then, especially in wars among Christians themselves, severe limitations were prescribed. War might be virtuous under certain conditions, but in any case, good or bad, one must sometimes abstain from it at any cost. The truce of God in the 10th century forbade fighting on holy days and in holy seasons. The hesitation and ambivalence of the Christian warrior are reflected in a curious oath of Robert the Pious (10th century) who wrote: "I will not take a mule or a horse . . . in pasture from any man from the kalends of March to the Feast of All Saints, unless to recover a debt. I will not burn houses or destroy them unless there is a knight inside. I will not root up vines. I will not attack noble ladies traveling without husband, nor their maids, nor widows or nuns unless it is their fault. From the beginning of Lent to the end of Easter, I will not attack an armed knight."*

It is easy to find texts like these which bring out the ridiculous inner inconsistencies that are inseparable from this view of war and the constant temptation to evade and rationalize the demands of the just war theory. The twofold weakness of the Augustinian theory is its stress on a subjective purity of intention which can be doctored and

* Quoted in Bainton, op. cit., p. 110.

manipulated with apparent "sincerity" and the tendency to pessimism about human nature and the world, now used as a *justification* for recourse to violence. Robert the Pious is characteristically naive when he blandly assumes that traveling nuns might at any moment be "at fault" and give a knight such utterly intolerable provocation that he would "have to attack them"—with full justice. Expanded to the megatonic scale, and viewing as licit the destruction of whole cities which are suddenly wicked and "at fault," this reasoning is no longer amusing.

We are told that Hitler, viewing the terrible conflagration of Warsaw when it had been bombed by the Luftwaffe, wept and said: "How wicked those people were to make me do this to them!"

4. THE LEGACY OF MACHIAVELLI

It seems likely that the doctrine of the just war and the moral inhibitions it implied did, at times, restrain barbarity in medieval war. We know that when the crossbow was invented it was at first banned by the Church as an immoral and cruel weapon.

However, in the Renaissance we find Machiavelli, one of the Fathers of *Realpolitik,* frankly disgusted with the half-heartedness and inefficiency with which wars were being carried on by certain Princes. It is instructive to read his grammar of power, *The Prince,* and to see how his pragmatic, not to say cynical, doctrine on the importance and the conduct of war are precisely those which are accepted in practice today in the international power struggle. It is difficult to say whether many of the more belligerent policy makers of our time have read Machiavelli, but one feels that he would be a man after their own heart: one who tolerates no nonsense about a sentimental and half-hearted use of force.

As Machiavelli is indifferent to moral considerations, we can say that he implicitly discards the theory of the just war as irrelevant. And in a sense one can agree with his evident contempt for all the absurd mental convolutions that Robert the Pious had to go through to provide escape clauses for his belligerent needs. It is certainly more practical, if what you intend is war, simply to go ahead and wage war without first vowing not to fight and then creating exceptional cases in which your vow is no longer binding. Surely we can agree that this is a great waste of time and energy and it may lead to fatal errors and to defeat. In a world of power politics, there is no question that conscience is a nuisance. But it is also true that in *any situation,* a conscience that juggles with the law and seeks only to rationalize evasions, is not only a nuisance but a fatal handicap, because it is basically unreasonable.

One might almost say that the present power struggle presents man with two clear alternatives: we can be true to the logic of our situation in two ways—either by discarding conscience altogether and acting with pure ruthlessness, or else by purifying our conscience and sharpening it to the point of absolute fidelity to moral law and Christian love. In the first case we will probably destroy one another. In the second, we may stand a chance of survival. Such at least is the teaching of Pope John.

The Prince, says Machiavelli, should have "no other aim or thought but war." He should reflect that disarmament would only render him contemptible. And in order to guard against temptation to relax his vigilance and reconcile himself to peace, the Prince must learn how not to be too good:

A man who wishes to make profession of goodness in everything must necessarily come to grief among so many who are not good. Therefore it is necessary for a Price who wishes to maintain himself to learn how not to be good, and to use this knowledge and not use it, according to the necessity of the case.

(*The Prince,* Ricci-Vincent Trans. c. 15)

After all, the Prince must be practical. Not only must he create a suitable image of himself, as we would say today: not only must he be feared rather than loved (unless he is smart enough to be both loved and feared at the same time), but he must be feared with very good reason. He must not listen to conscience, or to humane feeling. He must not practice virtue when it is not expedient to do so, and he must not let himself be either too kind, too generous, or too trustworthy. Let him not waste time abiding by legalities or by his pledged word, unless it happens to be useful. Virtue, Machiavelli warns, has ruined many a prince. It is better to rely on force.

There are two methods of fighting, the one by law and the other by force: The first method is that of men, the second of beasts; but as the first method is often insufficient, one must have recourse to the second. It is well then for a prince to know well how to use both the beast and the man.

This is the kind of practicality that is taken for granted but seldom stated so clearly in our age of power. It is refreshing to see it set forth with such primitive and pleasant frankness, free from all doubletalk. Machiavelli goes on to justify this line of conduct, with reasons which constitute in their own way a kind of "humanism." Cruelty, he says, is after all more merciful than an indulgent softness which leads only to disorder and chaos in the long run. Better to be firm like Cesare Borgia. (Machiavelli has nothing but praise for the Borgias.)

Cesare Borgia was considered cruel, but his cruelty had brought order to the Romagna, united it, and reduced it to peace and fealty. If this is considered evil, it will be seen that he was in reality much more merciful than the Florentine people who, to avoid the name of cruelty, allowed Pistoria to be destroyed. (*Id*. C. 17)

This is exactly the argument we hear today. The only hope of peace and order, according to "realists" is the toughest, hardest and most intransigent policy. This in the long run is "merciful" and peaceful.

Incidentally, Machiavelli was not praising simply the *appearance* of cruelty, although this is a necessary minimum. He thought that one of the chief qualities of Hannibal had been his genuine inhumanity. It really kept his army together!

While St Augustine transferred the question of war into the internal forum and concentrated on the intention of the Christian to wage a just war, Machiavelli ignores the forum of conscience as completely irrelevant. He is concerned with the brute objective facts of the power-struggle—a struggle in which conscience generates only ambivalence and therefore leads to defeat. Morality interferes with efficiency, therefore it is absurd to concern oneself with moral questions which in any case are practically meaningless, since the vicissitudes of the power-struggle may demand at any moment that they be thrown aside as useless baggage.

For Machiavelli power is an end in itself. Persons and policies are means to that end. And the chief means is war, not a "just" war but a *victorious* war. For Machiavelli the important thing was to *win*. As Clausewitz was to say in our modern age of *realpolitik: "To introduce into the philosophy of war a principle of moderation would be absurd. War is an act of violence pursued to the uttermost."*

And this of course was a philosophy which guided the policies of Hitler. The rest of the world, for all its good intentions, was forced to learn it from Hitler in order to beat him.

With modern technology the principles of unlimited destruction and violence has become in practice axiomatic. Deputy Defense Secretary of the U.S. Roswell Gilpatric, declared in 1961: "We are not going to reduce our nuclear capability. Personally I have never believed in a limited nuclear war. I do not know how you would build a limit into it when you use any kind of a nuclear bang."

Yet Machiavelli was not altogether typical of

the Renaissance. Leonardo da Vinci, the exemplar of Renaissance genius, developed a plan for a submarine but destroyed the plan without making it known because he saw that the only serious purpose of an underwater craft would be treacherous and hidden attack in naval war. In his mind, this was immoral.

While *The Prince* is a clear and articulate expression of the principles of power politics, we must be careful not to assume that the present power-struggle is purely and simply Machiavellian. This would be a grave error.

On the contrary, it is reasonable to suppose that in our day Machiavelli would have proceeded on different and more original assumptions, for this is no longer an age of warring princes of Italian city-states. He would doubtless be able to see through the romantic mythology with which the power-struggle has been invested (for instance the ideas of proletarian, nationalist or racist messianism) and he would certainly recognize the importance of rational control over the vast technological developments which, in fact, dominate our policies.

Machiavelli wrote his advice for the individual monarch, in a day when men believed in the divine right of kings. But after Machiavelli, political thought underwent considerable evolution. The "Prince" was replaced by the "Sov-

ereign State," and the revolutions which sought
to liberate man from the tyranny of absolute
monarchs brought them under the more subtle and
more absolute tyranny of an abstraction. Just as
mathematics, business and technology needed the
discovery of zero in order to develop, so too political
and economic power needed the faceless abstrac-
tions of state and corporation, with their unlimited
irresponsibility, to attain to unlimited sovereignty.
Hence the paradox that in the past ages usually
regarded as times of slavery the individual actually
counted for much more than he does in the alienation of modern economic, military and political
totalism. At the same time it is the modern,
irresponsible, faceless, alienated man, the man
whose thinking and decisions are the work of an
anonymous organization, who becomes the perfect
instrument of the power process. Under such conditions, the process itself becomes totally self-
sufficient and all absorbing. As a result the life and
death not only of individual persons, families and
cities, but of entire nations and civilizations must
submit to the blind force of amoral and inhuman
forces. The "freedom" and "autonomy" of a
certain minority may still seem to exist: it consists in little more than understanding the direction of the historically predetermined current and
rowing with the stream instead of against it. There

should be no need to point out the demonic potentialities of such a situation.

These summary notes on Machiavelli are of course oversimplified to the point of being naive. They are not intended as a critical or historical evaluation of his political philosophy, but only as a typology of popular notions about "Machiavellianism." This is a philosophy which England and America have traditionally regarded as villainous, and hence it would not be fair to blame even a Machiavellian typology for moral eccentricities that have other formal causes.

Machiavelli, who wanted to be ruthless, was actually leading a dull and rather innocuous life, and wrote his wicked book in the hope that it would get him a steady job under a powerful protector. In the atmosphere of a more northern morality, it sometimes happens that the same practical ruthlessness has been propounded with the air of greater respectability. Certainly the radical naturalism and secularism of Hobbes is just as uncompromising in its rejection of the possible ambiguities and sentimentalities of the too tender conscience. For Hobbes, the root of morality is obedience to the all-powerful despotic state and to the law of self-preservation and pleasure. The selfish interests of the individual are regulated by the power of the state. The Law of Nature, for Hobbes, is simply the "primitive and brutish" law of battle in which the strong overwhelm the weak, and this is kept under control by the force of that despotic Leviathan, the state, maintaining order by force. This confusion between the natural law considered as rooted in the essence of man as a free and rational being, and natural law as an empirical and primitive state of fact, interpreted moreover in crude and pessimistic terms, has had very serious consequences. (See Maritain, *Moral Philosophy*, p. 94) It has undoubtedly exercised some effect on Christian moralists in America without their realizing it perhaps, since Hobbes has contributed something to our national moral climate of rugged individualism.

So, too, of course, have Bentham and Mill. Here again the concept of nature as the basis of morality becomes more and more statistical, secularist and hedonistic. Mercantile calculation of the "greatest happiness of the greatest number" finally eroded away the last traces of the good as what was right and just in itself, and substituted for it the concept of the good as the advantageous. Justice was then replaced by "good business," and though the image of good business had and retains a specious folksiness, it is certainly no less ruthless and no less cynical in its roots than the political thought of Machiavelli. When it is optimistic, it remains a thoroughly inferior and jejune morality. When pessimistic, it legitimates any injustice as long as you don't get caught, or as long as you can get the courts on your side. In either event it represents a rather degraded concept of man, for all its seemingly humanistic slogans.

Kant's effort to put morality back on a firm basis of pure duty did not in fact restore a healthy climate of moral thought. The Kantian ethic easily degenerates into pietistic sentimentalities or moral platitudes. And after Kant came confusion: Hegel's emphasis on the power of the state in the face of the "prodigious power of the Negative," and other implicit philosophies of force. The Marxian dialectic of historical determinism, its humanism without the human person, leaves man powerless to transcend the forces of the social process in which he is immersed. Positivism is, once again, and even more than Bentham and Mill, statistical, amoral, a pointless and vapid sociologism. But it has had a profound effect in shaping "moral" thought in the climate of "free enterprise." One wonders how Christian thinkers, who are outraged by the Kinsey Report's approach to sexual morality, are so eager to accept a no less amoral and statistical approach to other crucial problems when it is made by Herman Kahn and the men with computers.

5. THE REPLY OF ''PACEM IN TERRIS''

Machiavelli devotes an extraordinary intelligence to the service of the prince's will to power, and is concerned with the inner dynamics of the struggle to subdue all rivals without concern for the means used except in so far as they obey the pragmatic laws of the struggle itself. His advice is certainly "rational," "intelligent" and even in a certain sense "scientific" and yet when it is considered on a deeper level it is seen to be utterly without rationality. It leads to ruinous consequences. The moralist who would seek, by accepting the moral climate and the premises of Machiavelli, to find a basis for distinctions between right and wrong within this program of power and to outline a morally licit use of the means and techniques suggested by the author of the Prince, might perhaps succeed, if he had sufficient casuistical ingenuity. If he were concerned only with the individual spiritual guidance of the Prince, his project might be viewed with tolerance and even with a certain sympathy. But we must consider that the actions of the Prince in obtaining power for himself do not concern himself alone, they affect the whole of society. And while the

Prince may be cleverly reconciling his ascent to power with the demands of a rather relaxed morality, others may be paying with their fortunes and with their lives for the luxury of his "good conscience."

The encyclical *Pacem in Terris* is not concerned with casuistry because it is not laying down norms merely for the individual "case." In fact the perspectives of individualism are not those of Pope John. It is true that the basis of the whole argument in *Pacem in Terris* is to be sought in the rights and dignity of the human person, but we must distinguish between *person* and *individual*. The individual can be considered as an isolated human unit functioning and acting for himself and by himself. The person can never be properly understood outside the framework of social relationships and obligations, for the person exists not merely in order to fight for survival: not only to function efficiently, and overcome others in competition for the goods of this earth which are thought to guarantee happiness. The person finds his reason for existence in the realm of truth, justice, love and liberty. He fulfils himself not by closing himself within the narrow confines of his own individual interests and those of his family, but by his openness to other men, to the civil society in which he lives and to the society of nations in which he is called to collaborate with others in building a world of security and peace.

If the person is to function rationally as a member of society, he must meet others on a common ground of reason. Common decisions and efforts which must be oriented toward the universal common good. This raises the question of arbitration when differences and disagreements arise. Hence one of the most important aspects of *Pacem in Terris* is its discussion of authority, its open criticism of the current failures of authority in the national and international sphere, and its demand for the formation of a valid supra-national authority with real power to arbitrate between nations and to deal fairly with the problems and needs of all.

Authority in Machiavelli rests on force and ruse, ruthlessness and cruelty, the ability to seize power and hold on to it against all contenders. This viewpoint, which is in practice quite commonly shared today, is not as "realistic" as it seems. It is actually a very unreal concept of authority. The authority of the strongest is no authority at all because it has no power to elicit the intelligent submission of man's inmost personal being. Authority cannot be properly understood if it is confused with mere external compulsion, supported by force.

Authority in *Pacem in Terris* rests on the objective reality of man, on the natural law, that is on the inner orientation of man to freedom, and on the obligations which this entails. The Legislator "is never allowed to depart from natural law" (*Pacem in Terris*, n. 81, 85. For the rest of this chapter, numbers otherwise not identified refer simply to paragraphs of *Pacem in Terris*)

The Legislator, in Pope John's eyes, should not be a ruthless and clever operator with unlimited power at his disposal, justified in taking any decision that serves him and his party or nation in the power-struggle. He must be a "man of great equilibrium and integrity" (71) competent and courageous, prompt to take decisions which respond to the situation and of the principles that are at stake. And he must not evade his basic moral obligations for "reasons of state." On the contrary, statesmen and governments which put their own interests before everything else, including justice and the natural law, are no better than bandits.

As men in their private enterprises cannot pursue their own interests to the detriment of others, so too states cannot lawfully seek that development of their own resources which brings harm to other states and unjustly oppresses them. This statement of St Augustine seems to be very apt in this regard: What are kingdoms without justice but large bands of robbers? (92)

At the same time, the Pope condemns all isolationism and nationalist individualism which might prompt a government to seek its own interests, ignoring and contemning the rest of the world. At the present time all the countries in the world are in fact so closely interrelated that no one nation can simply turn in upon itself and seek its own advantage without affecting the others. Hence "it is obvious that individual countries cannot seek their own interests and development in isolation from the rest." (131)

Pope John tirelessly repeats the principle that *force is not and cannot be a valid basis of public authority:*

A civil authority that uses as its only or chief means either threats and fear of punishment or promises of rewards cannot effectively move men to promote the common good of all. (48)

For that reason (both men and nations) are right in not easily yielding obedience to authority imposed by force or to an authority in whose creation they had no part, and to which they themselves did not decide to submit by their own free choice. (138)

If force is not the basis of authority, then what is? Reason and conscience. The "free choice" made by men in accepting authority is of course something more than a whim of fashion. Men do not necessarily accept authority because they are pleased by all its manifestations. But it is right and just to accept a rule of authority that obeys truth, guarantees men's rights, and recommends itself to free men by its respect for liberty. "Civil authority must appeal primarily to the conscience of individual citizens, that is to each one's duty to collaborate readily for the common good of all." (48) Authority can exercise a righful appeal to the consciences of men in so far as it offers them some convincing indication that it can provide them with an ordered and productive life, with liberty and the advantages of a peaceful culture. But ultimately this pragmatic assurance which may be deduced from the successful working of authority, is only a sign of the moral order from which its derives its obligatory force. (47) The "ultimate source and final end of all authority" is God Himself. (47)

Incidentally, this shows why Pope John is so intent on preserving the independent authority of the small and struggling nation, so that it may settle its own internal affairs without interference from more powerful neighbors.

No country may unjustly oppress others or unduly meddle in their affairs. On the contrary all should help to develop in others a sense of responsibility, a spirit of enterprise, and an earnest desire to be the first to promote their own advancement in every field. (120)

Since all authority ultimately rests on God Himself, a civil or international authority which promotes policies contrary to the moral order thereby renounces its right to be obeyed, for "God is to be obeyed rather than men." (51) (cf. Acts 5:29) *Pacem in Terris* declares frankly and clearly that "Those therefore who have authority in the State may oblige men in conscience only if their authority is intrinsically related to the authority of God and shares in it." (49)

It follows that if civil authorities pass laws or command anything opposed to the moral order and consequently contrary to the will of God, neither the laws made nor the authorization granted can be binding on the consciences of the citizens. (The Pope then quotes St. Thomas, after referring to Acts 5:29) "In so far as it falls short of right reason a law is said to be a wicked law; and so lacking the true nature of law it is rather a kind of violence." (I II Q. 93, a.3, ad.2) (51)

It should, by the way, be clear from the context of the encyclical that when the Pope speaks of civil authority being "intrinsically related to the authority of God" he is in no way saying that a quasi-religious and clerical form of society has more authority than any other. *Pacem in Terris,* as everyone well knows who understands the language of John XXIII and its background in St Thomas, is by no means a tract in favor of theocracy. The Pope takes pains to point out that he is speaking of "any truly democratic regime" (52) chosen by the people themselves in a free and just manner. There is even some basis for respecting the claims of a government which represents "men of no Christian faith whatever but who are endowed with reason and adorned with a natural uprightness of conduct." (157) This does not imply that false ideologies are approved, but if men following these ideologies are justly and sincerely striving to improve the lot of their people, they retain certain rights in the eyes of the natural law and of God. Their legitimate efforts to improve their living conditions should be aided, not hindered by other nations.

This principle is very important when we come to consider the revolutions that mark the emergence of new nations and new societies, and will continue to do so especially in Latin America, Africa and Asia. Pope John warns that superior strength does not warrant interference in the affairs of small states even though the "revolutionary" character of the social ferment may not be acceptable to those more advanced and more highly civilized powers. "This superiority, far from permitting (an advanced nation) to rule others unjustly, imposes the obligation to make a greater contribution to the general development of the people." (88) In this context, Pope John condemns all forms of racism (86, 94, 95) and explicitly points to genocide as a flagrant crime against humanity. (95)

To sum this all up in one word: Pope John teaches that when authority ignores natural law human dignity, human rights and the moral order established by God, it undermines it own foundations and loses its claim to be obeyed because it no longer speaks seriously to the conscience of free man. One very serious consequence flows from this teaching: One of the great collective questions of conscience of our time is, according to Pope John the failure of authority to cope with the critical needs and desperate problems of man on a world scale. A truly international authority is the only answer, and the establishment of a genuine world community is "urgently demanded today by the requirements of the universal common good." (7)

Today the universal common good poses problems of world-wide dimensions which cannot be adequately tackled or solved except by the efforts of public authority . . . on a world-wide basis. The moral order itself demands that such a form of authority be established. (137)

What is the reason? The Pope does not hesitate to tell us:

Under the present circumstances of humanity both the structure and form of governments as well as the power which public authority wields in all the nations of the world MUST BE CONSIDERED INADEQUATE TO PROMOTE THE UNIVERSAL COMMON GOOD. (135)

If we understand the nature of this document and its profound seriousness, we can see that certain deeply Christian obligations begin to emerge from the world crisis in which we live. The obligation to work for collaboration and harmony among nations, to respect the rights of small and emergent nations and of racial minorities, to collaborate actively and generously in helping these nations and races to attain their full development and to enjoy their full rights as members of the human race. The obligation to work for peace and the need for a clear and forthright protest of the Christian conscience against the abuse of authority which marshals men more and more under the command of those who explicitly announce their intention to make use of brute force in order to gain or to maintain a position of power for themselves or for the social and political system which they represent.

All this implies a willing and intelligent participation of the Christian in civil and public life, to the extent that it fits in with his other duties. (7, 137)

To say that authority has its source in God

is then to say that it begins and ends in liberty. It exists for the sake of liberty. It is the servant of liberty, and when it ceases to be the servant of liberty in the highest sense it loses its power to command the obedience of the free conscience. For man is made free in the image and likeness of God and social authority exists only to help him use his freedom in truth, love and justice as a child of God. This is all new and strange, no doubt, to those who have become accustomed to exhortations to obedience in a quite other context, where authority seems to be rooted only in the *power to compel obedience by external force* or by the law of fear. But that concept of authority, Pope John reminds us, is not the Christian concept. It is in fact closer to Machiavelli than it is to the Gospel because it fits into the framework of a power structure dominated by arbitrary will, rather than an intelligent order tending toward the full development of freedom in justice and love.

We can now begin to see why an Encyclical of Peace on Earth actually devotes so much thought to the true nature of authority within the order of justice and love, which is the order of freedom into which we are called by the very fact that we are persons created in the image and likeness of God. And we see that the real difference between the authority of love and truth, taught by Pope John, and the authority of brute force, implies totally different concepts of man and of the world. And when we grasp this difference we see how it happens that so many "right thinking men" often end up with an ideology of authority based on force (analogous to that of Machiavelli) and fail to grasp the Christian need for an authority of freedom and love.

The difference of course is this: the totalitarian and absolute concept of authority based on force implies a completely pessimistic view of man and of the world. It is for one reason or another implicitly closed to human values, distrustful or openly contemptuous of reason, fearful of liberty which it cannot distinguish from licence and rebellion. It seeks security in force because it cannot believe that the powers of nature, if left to grow spontaneously, can develop in a sane and healthy fashion. Nature must be controlled with an iron hand because it is evil, or prone to evil: man is perhaps capable of good behavior, but only if he is forced into it by implacable authority. We find this idea cropping up in all kinds of contexts, religious or otherwise, from Calvin to Stalin, from Port Royal to Hitler; there are traces of it in Plato and in St Augustine; we see it in Fathers of the Church like Tertullian; it provides specious reasons for the Inquisition as well as for Auschwitz. It is in Machiavelli of course, in a slightly different form (Machiavelli is not concerned over anyone being "good," but his philosophy of ruthlessness implies that the law of fear is the only one that can be relied upon to keep men under control).

Pope John was opposed, and passionately opposed, to this kind of pessimism which he diagnosed as a sickness akin to despair, masking as strength and rectitude, but in reality refusing a generous response to the grace and the call of God to twentieth century Christians. Against the triumphalist hopes which exalt the Church by placing an authoritarian heel on the neck of prostrate man, Pope John dared to hope in the goodness placed in human nature by God the Creator. Only if human nature is radically good can a concept of authority based on the natural law and on human liberty be conceived as also at the same time rooted in the will of God. If human nature is evil, then obviously all God-given authority has no other function than to take up arms against it, to restrict it, punish it and imprison it in blind and disciplined servitude.

Indeed, if human nature is evil, the question of peace and war and the authority of nations and of the Church comes to be seen in a different light. If man is evil, then it is obvious that he will tend to destroy himself by fighting greedily for his own advantage. War is therefore inevitable, because the struggle for power is inescapable. *This* indeed is the law of nature! The supernatural au-

thority of the Church must then save man in spite
of himself by making him obey the authority of
"the right side" in this blind conflict for power.
And fortunately the Church still has enough
power to demand his submission! She must preserve her power so that wicked man may have a
supernatural authority to which he may submit . . .

This is not Pope John's conception of authority,
of man or of the order of salvation!

It is easy to see that Pope John's ideas go back
to the optimism of St Paul and of the Gospels. St
Paul in moving passages outlines the great mystery
of the whole cosmos redeemed in Christ, the new
creation.

For the eager longing of creation awaits the revelation of the sons of God. For creation was made subject
to vanity—not by its own will but by reason of him who
made it subject—in hope, because creation itself also
will be delivered from its slavery to corruption into the
freedom of the glory of the sons of God. For we know
that all creation groans and travails in pain until now.
And not only it, but we ourselves also who have the
first-fruits of the Spirit—we ourselves groan within
ourselves, waiting for the adoption as sons, the redemption of our body.

Romans 8:19–23

He is the image of the invisible God, the firstborn
of every creature. For in him were created all things in
the heavens and on the earth, things visible and things

invisible, whether Thrones, or Dominations, or Princi-
palities, or Powers. All things have been created through
and unto him, and he is before all creatures, and in him
all things hold together. Again, he is the head of his
body, the Church; he, who is the beginning, the firstborn from the dead, that in all things he may have the
first place. For it has pleased God the Father that in
him all his fullness should dwell, and that through him
he should reconcile to himself all things, whether on
earth or in the heavens, making peace through the blood
of his cross.

(*Colossians* 1:15–20)

Pope John also echoes the optimism of St
Thomas Aquinas who was regarded as a revolutionary in the thirteenth century because of the
bold scope of his vision which united the created
and the uncreated, nature and grace, reason and
faith in a vast unity. St Thomas gave the Church
his great unified theology in a period when the
division between earth and heaven, nature and
supernature, philosophy and theology, reason and
faith, had become so acute that they threatened
to become irreconcilable. His task, as Joseph Pieper
sees it, was this:

A "legitimate union" would mean two things. First
it would mean joining the two realms so that their dis-
tinctiveness and irreducibility, their relative autonomy,
their intrinsic justification, were seen and recognized.
Second it would mean making their unity, their com-
patibility, and the necessity for their conjunction ap-

parent not from the point of view of either of the two members of the union—neither simply from the point of view of faith nor simply from the point of view of reason—*but by going back to a deeper root of both*. (*Guide to Thomas Aquinas*, p. 120)

Caught between radical Averroism (which was frankly rationalistic) and the conservative supernaturalism of those who could not accept Aristotle and so fell back on traditional positions, rejecting reason and "the world," St Thomas dared to transcend them both and to demonstrate the natural goodness of the world as something that could not be fully understood and vindicated except in the light of the revealed doctrine of creation.

Things are good—*all* things. The most compelling proof of their goodness in the very act of being lies in their createdness; there is no more powerful argument for affirmation of natural reality of the world than the demonstration that the world is *creatura* . . . Sin, whether on the part of the angels or on the part of men, cannot essentially have changed the structure of the world. Therefore, Thomas argues, I refuse to consider the present state of the world as a basically unnatural state, a state of denaturalization. What is, is good because it was created by God; whoever casts aspersions upon the perfections of created beings casts aspersions upon the perfection of the divine power. (Pieper, op. cit., p. 131)

The optimism of Pope John is not the vapid and sentimental cheerfulness of a pseudo naturalistic religiosity. Yet it embraces all the best hopes and intuitions of the modern world of science and technology, and unites them with the spiritual vision of Christianity. The union is reached, as was that of St Thomas's *Summa,* by going to a "deeper root."

Let us be perfectly clear about the optimism of *Mater et Magistra* and *Pacem in Terris.* Pope John is not *excusing* nature, or tolerantly *defending* nature. He is not saying that humanity is not so bad after all, and that there is a chance for it to act as if it were good, once it has been brought into line by the wisely applied will of an external power. As Pieper said of St Thomas, so we can say of Pope John: "to his mind it would be utterly ridiculous for man to undertake to defend the creation. Creation needs no justification. The order of creation is, on the contrary, precisely the standard which must govern man's every judgement of things and of himself." (*Id.* p. 122)

This truth rings out clearly in the very first line of *Pacem in Terris* where Pope John declares that all men desire peace and that "it can be established only if the order laid down by God be dutifully observed." That order is the law implanted in man's free nature as an intelligent being who is capable of desiring peace in justice and of being a peace-maker in the fulness of love. These very capacities implanted in his nature by God are the sign of man's radical goodness, the guarantee of his honest hopes, the challenge which his intelligence and love are summoned to meet, the "law" of his nature which is made in the image and likeness of a loving God. Pope John's optimism lies in this belief: that because man was made by God to seek peace and to achieve it, and because God has given man the abundant help of supernatural grace, then no matter how great man's confusion and servitude to evil may have become, he can still be liberated and fulfil his vocation in peace as a free, spiritual being redeemed in the blood of Christ.

The pessimist view, on the contrary, considers man's aspiration to peace to be at best a delusive hope which can be exploited by any kind of power: the evil power that enslaves him or the benevolent paternal power that leads him blindly, like a helpless child, and almost in spite of himself, to heaven.

The pessimistic view is closed, inattentive to man's desperate aspirations for peace, social justice, progress, change. It tells man that these are simply manifestations of pride and naturalism. Let him learn to be resigned to war on earth and peace in heaven! The optimism of Pope John is wide open to every legitimate hope of man for peace *on earth!* It is willing to listen to any reasonable plan, and to share any worthy human desire. It is willing to discuss possibilities of agreement even with those who do not believe in God and who reject the truths of faith and the world of the spirit, for the "acceptance of all natural reality necessarily involves the acceptance of valuable insights wherever they may be found—and therefore also in the pre-Christian and extra Christian worlds." (Pieper, op. cit., 125)

The great difference between Pope John and Machiavelli is not that the Pope believed in God and Machiavelli did not (as far as I know Machiavelli was, in his own way, a "practising Catholic") but rather that Pope John believed *in man* and Machiavelli did not. Because he had confidence in man, Pope John believed in love and peace. Because he lacked this confidence, Machiavelli believed in force and in deceit.

The power for peace in this great Encyclical resides then not in a casuistical treatment of the problem of nuclear war but in the profound and optimistic Christian spirit with which the Pope lays bare the deepest roots of peace, roots which are placed in man by God Himself and which man himself has the mission to cultivate. If the roots of peace are not in our hearts, it would be useless to condemn total war over and over again with ecclesiastical anathemas. But because the roots of peace are there, it makes sense for the Church to remind us of the fact in all simplicity and to tell us about them, adding at the same time:

There can be, or at least there should be, no doubt that relations between states as between individuals should be regulated not by the force of arms but by the light of reason, by the rule that is of truth, of justice, and of active and sincere cooperation. (144)

In an age such as ours which prides itself on its atomic energy it is contrary to reason to hold that war is now a suitable way to restore rights that have been violated. (127)

One last remark about the encyclical: without being in any sense a professional Thomist, the Pope reflects everywhere the principles and sanity of Aquinas. But the whole climate of the encyclical, in its love of man and of the world, and in its radiant hopefulness, is Franciscan. The optimism of Pope John is not logical only: it is spiritual, mystical, rooted in a deep and simple love for God which is also, love for His creation and for God's child: man.

Anyone familiar with the writings of St Francis and with his life is aware that the Saint was always urging his Friars to be at peace with each other and to go among men as peacemakers. A remarkable chapter on missions among the Saracens (First Rule of St Francis, C. 16) anticipates the ecumenical ideas of our own time, even though it was written in the age of crusades:

There are two ways in which the friars who go out (to the Saracens) can act with spiritual effect. The first is not to dispute or be contentious, but for love of the Lord to bow to every human authority and to acknowledge themselves Christians. The other way, whenever they think it to be God's will, is to proclaim the Word of God and then faith in God Almighty, the Father, the Son and the Holy Spirit . . .

All friars everywhere are to remember that they have given and surrendered themselves soul and body to our Lord Jesus Christ and for love of Him they must expose themselves to all enemies both visible and invisible, for our Lord says: "The man who loses his life for my sake shall save it in life everlasting."

And we know that St Francis, toward the end of his life, made peace between the Mayor and Bishop at Assisi by sending one of the friars to sing his wonderful hymn in praise of God in His creatures in their presence. He thought (as did Pope John) that the best way to turn men's minds to peace was to remind them of the goodness of life and of the world. The friar came, sang the "Song of Brother Sun," to which St Francis had added two lines, about peace. The mayor listened in tears. The bishop confessed his own haughtiness. And there was peace between them.

This is a charming story. No doubt we will need more than charming stories to bring peace to the world of our time. But the meaning is there: where there is a deep, simple, all-embracing love of man, of the created world of living and inanimate things, then there will be respect for life, for freedom, for truth, for justice and there will be humble love of God. But where there is no love of man, no love of life, then make all the laws you want, all the edicts and treaties, issue all the anathemas; set up all the safeguards and inspections, fill the air with spying satellites, and hang cameras on the moon. As long as you see your fellow man as a being essentially to be feared, mistrusted, hated, and destroyed, there cannot be peace on earth. And who knows if fear alone will suffice to prevent a war of total destruction? Pope John was not among those who believe that fear is enough.

June 1964.

THE CHRISTIAN IN THE DIASPORA

I. RAHNER'S DIASPORA

It is no secret that the Church finds herself in crisis, and the awareness of such a fact is "pessimism" only in the eyes of those for whom all change is necessarily a tragedy. It would seem more realistic to follow the example of Pope John (and of Pope Paul after him) and to face courageously the challenges of an unknown future in which the Christian can find security not, perhaps, in the lasting strength of familiar human structures but certainly in the promises of Christ and in the power of the Holy Spirit. After all, Christian hope itself would be meaningless if there were no risks to face and if the future were definitively mortgaged to an unchanging present.

Christian hope is confidence not in metaphysical immobility but in the dynamism of unfailing love. "Crisis" means "judgement," and the present is always being judged as it gives way to what was, yesterday, the future. Only when we try to drag yesterday bodily with us into the future does "crisis" become "cataclysm." An "optimism" that insists on denying evident realities is hardly inspired by Christian truth, and true hope is that which finds motives for confidence precisely in the "crisis" which seems to threaten that which is dearest to us: for it is here above all that the power of God will break through the meaningless impasse of prejudices and cruelties in which we always tend to become entrapped. It is in the crises of history most of all that the Church knows, from experience, that the truth shall make her free.

The life of St Fronto, apostle of an obscure corner of southwestern France, relates (without a shadow of historical foundation) that the Emperor who had exiled Fronto to that forsaken spot with numerous companions, was moved to pity and sent seventy camels there laden with provisions for them. Once when this story was being narrated in a catechism class in St Fronto's town, Perigueux, one of the children asked why there were no camels to be seen in the neighborhood today. "My child," replied the Abbé, "we no longer deserve them."

This story rather neatly characterizes the resentments and frustrations which underlie a certain mood of conservative "triumphalism" in the Church. On one hand, everything said about the

Church by these defenders of the *status quo* is couched in the language of the victory communiqué (to borrow Hans Küng's apt phrase). Yet in the same breath dire prophecies and lamentations chime in to condemn the decadence, the "modernism," the "secularism" which have "utterly ruined" Catholicism and Christian culture today. Basic to this view is the assumption that medieval Christendom was a unique and timeless norm which we must work to reestablish. *Aggiornamento* does not mean preparing to assume the risks of an ill-defined and threatening future, but recovering the security and power of the glorious past. The proclamation of this "norm" accounts for the triumphal tone of their pronouncements. The unwilling recognition that it is a norm not likely to be met accounts for their gloom. The modern world, with its forgetfulness of the past and its contempt for ecclesiastical power and prestige, has ceased to deserve the glories and miracles of a better day. That is why there are no camels in Perigueux.

On the other hand there are theologians like Karl Rahner, supported by many other of his compatriots, both Protestant and Catholic, who believe that we must frankly face and accept what they have called the "diaspora situation" of the Church in the twentieth century. Speaking not as a sociologist but precisely as a theologian,

Rahner describes this situation as irreversible and concludes that we have no alternative but to accept it. He adds that this acceptance is not a matter of defeat or passive fatalism. On the contrary, he seeks to show, theologically, that it has a crucial significance for our salvation and for the salvation of the world. In a word, Rahner emphatically rejects an unrealistic optimism of the triumphalist type, which supposes that with a little more zeal, a little more energy, a few more mass movements and a smarter use of mass-media, the Church will very likely take over everything and definitively convert the City of Man into the City of God— on a medieval pattern. He is convinced, and perhaps with good reason, that the "diaspora situation" will make official clerical action increasingly difficult.

In the "diaspora situation" the Church will (and indeed already does) exist to a great extent as a stone of stumbling and a sign of contradiction. The faith of the individual Christian will be constantly menaced and insecure. The official apostolic activity of the clergy will be blocked and neutralized by the arbitrary whims of secular powers.

Yet the work of the Church in the world, and precisely in the secular sphere, will be carried on with ever greater dedication and effect, chiefly through the heroic and enlightened work of the laity. In a word, Rahner says, the Church will depend entirely on the good will and fervor of her ordinary members. The impact of the apostolate in such a situation will, he thinks, be very significant. It will be qualitative not quantitative, and it will draw strength not from a massive ecclesiastical assault organized on quasi-military lines, but on the openness, the freedom, the total sincerity with which the ordinary Christian is prepared to meet the non-Christian on his own ground and awaken him to the truth of the Gospel in terms that he can understand and accept. This means of course that the apostle of the diaspora will have to have something more cogent to offer than an invitation to enter a ghetto of antiquated customs, outworn rituals, and censorious theological rigidity. The only thing that can give meaning to such an apostolate is the purity of eschatalogical hope. In the light of that authentic hope, Rahner evaluates the triumphalist regression as a thinly veiled despair.

Karl Rahner's profound and controversial "Essays in pastoral theology"* represent a radical attempt by the distinguished Innsbruck theologian to face the "new tasks of the Church." At no point does the author engage in superficial or pragmatic diagnosis, nor does he at any time hopefully prescribe quick remedies for all our ills.

---

* *The Christian Commitment* by Karl Rahner, S.J. Translated by Cecily Hastings, Sheed & Ward, 218 pp.

On the contrary, no Catholic theologian has so squarely faced the critical seriousness of the Church's task in the modern world. From a certain viewpoint Rahner might seem to be a pessimist, for he sees no hope whatever of preserving the Church's medieval status, and of recovering for her a position of power and preeminence in modern society. Yet Rahner, like Kierkegaard before him, does not regard this solution as a valid Christian hope. It must be abandoned in favor of a *true* hope, hope not in "Catholic power" but in the eschatalogical victory of Christ.

Rahner's thesis is frank and it is one which many will find deeply disturbing. He is saying that Catholics cannot realistically hope to restore and maintain a kind of religio-cultural autonomy in the secular world today and that if we build our lives and our apostolate on the theory that Medieval Christendom is the norm for Christianity in the world, we are heading for trouble. He says, "It is never possible simply to deduce from Christian principles of belief and morality any one single pattern of the (secular) world as it ought to be" (p. 7). "Even in earlier times the particular concrete form given to the Christian ideal was not determined by Christianity as such (though indeed by Christians) but by other historical forces and influences. But it was possible in earlier times to *confuse* the original principles and the practice of them, with a particular ideal at work on the historical level and to regard this synthesis as final and obligatory" (p. 11). Hence we must face the fact that "we do not have a complete recipe for the world's problems in our pockets."

Does this mean that as Christians we take no interest in the problems of the world, and have no concern for them? That there is a complete fissure in our lives between the "sacred" and the "profane"? That we turn our back on secular society and pray to save our own souls while others perish? This is exactly what Rahner is not saying. When he denies that there is, or can be, one "official" and indubitable Christian approach to all economic, political and cultural matters, he wishes to throw open the way to a much more living, more varied and more creative Christian action in the world. There is a whole sphere of life where the Christian layman, precisely as Christian and as a responsible member of the Holy People of God, is called upon to take original and creative action in his own sphere. The principles to be followed are made plain on the "ecclesial" level, but the application should be left to the prudence of the individual Christian.

Thus the political action of the Christian does not become confused with projects centered around an official and clericalist "party line," nor

is it inevitably associated with the propagation of
a dogmatic message which the rest of the world is
not disposed to hear without challenging it. But
on the other hand this Christian action is concretely ordered to advancing the work of Redemption and deepening the penetration of grace into
the realm of society and nature. As Rahner says,
this Christian action, though not "ecclesial" is
nevertheless supernatural. It is "action of Christians but not action of the Church" (p. 43). This
particular field of Christian action belongs to the
layman, but it is not merely assigned to him as a
kind of token or consolation prize. It is his inalienable task as a Christian and if he does not do
it, nobody else will. Rahner says:

> The most strictly lay apostolate has its roots in the
> Church's order of reality but it is not an apostolate of
> the Church in the strict sense . . . The layman is, as
> an individual, irreplaceable, with a strictly Christian
> and moral task to be performed within groups not
> directly subject to the Church's official control a task
> of which he will have to give an account before the
> judgment seat of God. (p. 66)

If by "ecclesial" action we mean that Christian action by which the Church manifests
Christ in the world, then this is certainly not confined only to hierarchical and sacerdotal activity.
The Christian initiatives of the laity in so far as

they are Christian will also be a manifestation of Christ living and carrying on the mystery of redemption in and through his Church. It would seem that in restricting the term "ecclesial" to the strict sense of "official" Rahner would in the long run be going against the cogency of his own arguments. However we must see him in his own context.

Rahner wants to show that we must intervene in the social life of our world, and we must do so as Christians, guided by Christian principles, indeed moved and led by the Holy Spirit. But he also wants to make clear that we cannot propagate our social ideas precisely in the name of the Church, invoking her hierarchical authority. We tend to think that all loyalty to the Church demands explicit and aggressive assertion of her juridical authority even when this is irrelevant, or needlessly brings discredit upon the Church, or causes Christianity itself to be attacked for political reasons. "If we make some synthesis of Christian principles and our own historical preferences and then propagate that *as what Christianity unconditionally demands,* to stand or fall by it, then people will take us at our word in this false declaration. They will then unavoidably combat Christianity itself." (p. 11)

Rahner, speaking not as historian or sociologist but as a theologian declares not only that our present situation "can be characterized as that of a diaspora," (p. 14) but insists (and this is more important) that *theologically* we are obliged to accept this fact as the starting point for all conclusions about our behavior as Christians in the modern world. Our diaspora situation is then not simply an unavoidable evil, traceable to the infidelities of Christians and to the godlessness of neo-pagans and materialists. It is not just something we must put up with as "permitted" by the divine will for our testing. It is not a state of affairs which we can hope to reverse by a more earnest apostolate supported by greater purity and zeal. It is irreversible, and it is moreover a state of affairs, "a 'must' in terms of the history of salvation." (p. 14)

This is a strong statement. Rahner qualifies it. It is not what *ought to be,* (yet are we so sure that we know what ought to be?) and it is in fact in contradiction with what we would expect after the Gospel has been preached for two millennia. It is not something we can accept with passive fatalism. Rahner is not a quietist. Nor should we simply sit back with grim satisfaction and wait for the bomb to confirm our apocalyptic prognostication by wiping out the whole intolerable mess. We must accept the diaspora situation *as existing* and as certain to go on existing. It is not something "to be grimly endured and fought against," but it "has a significance for salvation." It is in fact a challenge and it offers an implicit promise of hope and of victory to courageous Christian faith.

This is a very radical pronouncement, but we must pay serious attention to it, since it is the kind of thinking that led Pope John XXIII to open a dialogue with the left. The wisdom of Pope John's action has of course been openly questioned by conservatives, some of whom have now become attached to a myth of a "good old Pope" who had romantic ideas but was definitely "not practical."

Are we to assume that Pope John ought to have looked at Russia in exactly the same way as Pius V looked at the Turk? Such an assumption, judged from Rahner's viewpoint, would sterilize all Christian action in the diaspora situation in which the Church is called upon not to seek coexistence at the price of compromise—far from it—but to pursue her historic task of redemption which is already "eschatalogically complete" but remains to be "fully realized through human beings." (p. 53) Rahner does not envisage any Christian revolution that will transform the world overnight into the City of God. The diaspora character of our age is (he believes) going to increase. "The new age of Jesus Christ, as prophesied by Lombardi is certainly not going to dawn for some considerable while (Rahner says). On the contrary, the Christendom of the Middle Ages and after

. . . is going to disappear with ever increasing speed. For the causes which have brought about this process in the west are still at work and have not yet had their full effect." (p. 17)

These evaluations of a historic situation may perhaps seem gratuitous, and they can certainly be disputed. Our purpose here is not to argue with Rahner, but to get a good clear look at his thesis and to understand it correctly. He is certainly not saying that Christian action in the world has no hope of achieving anything. On the contrary, he believes that it is absolutely essential, especially now, precisely because we are entering the *diaspora,* when "the Church's vital power and her salvational import for the world must be manifested" clearly and forcefully in the secular sphere. (p. 44) We cannot understand this unless we see that for Rahner the "world" and "secularity" or even the "profane" are not categories which by their very nature *exclude* and *obstruct* the action of grace. They are on the contrary fully embraced by the order of redemption and the world must be brought to an awareness of this by the heroic witness of Christian faith.

To admit that the diaspora situation is one where clerical action will be frustrated and impeded, and to accept this fact is not, for Rahner, to admit defeat. On the contrary, refusal to accept this means that the Church's energies in the diaspora will be dissipated in useless and frantic struggles to assert clerical authority where that assertion has relatively little apostolic meaning or usefulness, and where much greater good would be done by another approach.

We repeat, the "diaspora situation" is not one which Christians should desire, or even accept with gladness. We must indeed regret it. It is a situation which is deplorable because unfavorable to the Church, at least from a sociological viewpoint. However, there is more involved than sociology and we know from the Bible that hostility between the Church and her enemies is inevitable. It remains only for us to interpret this situation of conflict properly and take a genuinely Christian attitude. This demands faith in the promises of Christ that His Church will endure, and expectation of the combat, persecution, and ever more critical struggle in which "the victory of Christianity (will) not be the fruit of immanent development and . . . progressive leavening of the world (but will be) the act of God coming in judgment to gather up world history into its wholly unpredictable and unexpected end." (p. 19)

The diaspora situation is one then in which the Church is a stumbling block to the world, a sign of contradiction. In this situation the faith of the individual Christian is always threatened.

Considered from a sociological viewpoint, faith needs a favorable milieu in which to develop. Most individuals cannot preserve their faith intact if left alone with it in the midst of a hostile or indifferent society. He who realizes himself morally and spiritually isolated from his fellows gets the impression that he is abnormal and therefore guilty. (See *"Doutes dans la Vie de Foi"* under *Foi,* by André de Bovis, S.J. in *Dictionnaire de Spiritualité,* V col. 616) Yet in the diaspora situation the Christian as individual may precisely be asked a heroic faith with little or no human support. Vocation to the faith then becomes a desperate wager, because the Church is hindered in her (rightful) activities of preaching and teaching, and access to the Sacraments may be very irregular and uncertain. The clergy will no longer have a privileged social status. They will be more and more a despised or at least an unappreciated class. The "problem of Church and state" will have ceased practically to exist except in secret conflicts of the individual conscience. But here it may indeed be terribly acute, for the individual Christian will be simultaneously a member of Christ and a citizen of a perhaps godless society. Indeed, the one thing above all other that will characterize the Church in Rahner's "diaspora situation" will be the heroism and total dedication of those who take their faith seriously enough to remain Christians under such conditions. The Church will have no support from secular power, no subsidies, but will depend permanently "on the good will of her ordinary members." With all these obstacles the Church, even though to some extent reduced to silence, will *continue her missionary activity*, but now in radically new forms in which the purity of individual witness will take precedence over everything else. Not only will the Church continue to preach the Gospel, without defeatism and without rancor, she will *remain on the offensive*. But this "offensive" will be completely independent of human power relying, like that of the apostles, on the power of God.

In fact the word "offensive" is perhaps ill-chosen. It is not meant to suggest truculence and aggression. Rahner is talking about an attitude of openness, understanding, and sympathy which enables the Catholic to discover unsuspected values in a secular world which he has hitherto regarded only with mistrust and with contempt. Rahner is therefore not prescribing a resolute and para-military advance to "conquer" the world and bring it entirely into subjection under clerical influence or discipline. It is rather a positive and truly apostolic effort to encounter the non-Christian on his own ground in order to bring him the Gospel message, in a form in which he can best understand and receive it. But if we merely invite him to enter with us into a ghetto in which the spiritual atmosphere seems grimly opposed to everything he experiences as "life," he will turn away from us in despair.

2. THE MONK IN THE DIASPORA

Rahner's book is addressed mainly to lay-apostles. Has it any relevance for monastic Orders?

It is curious that the one saint singled out by Rahner for mention as an example of one who understood the diaspora situation is St Benedict. Without necessarily agreeing with the statement that St Benedict "reformed monasticism" (as if the copious monastic literature of fifth century Gaul did not give evidence of a rich pre-Benedictine monastic life in the West) we can profitably consider the author of the Benedictine Rule as one who, in a world which he saw was alien to his own ideals, nevertheless lived a fully Christian life which was fruitful beyond his own wildest expectations.

It is obvious that religious and clerical life will be considerably changed in the diaspora envisaged by Rahner. Indeed it may become unrecognizable and it is quite likely that many religious institutes will simply cease to exist. In any case, diaspora or no diaspora, there can be no question that the religious life faces a crisis today. Within the various Orders there is a climate of optimism, some of it naive, some perhaps well-founded. Among the monastic Orders there is some feeling that we may have better chances in a diaspora than other Orders, since we are, or should be, less dependent on official and institutional structures and on the support of the outside world.

The monk lives, at least theoretically, a contemplative life in which active works play only an incidental part or none at all. Provided he is allowed to work the land and make his own living, the monk can survive where schools are closed, the Catholic press is suppressed and other institutions are taken out of Catholic hands. There is no real need for the monk to be a cleric or a priest, and traditionally the monk is in fact not a cleric. The earliest monks were simply laymen living in solitude or in small informal communities of a somewhat charismatic nature, grouped around a holy and well tried hermit, a "spiritual father." So, traditionally, the monastic life does not require much organization. Strictly speaking there is no reason why a group of men should not buy a farm in some remote part of Canada and simply live there as monks (with the proper permissions) minding their own business and devoting themselves to work and prayer in a small eschatalogical community like those of the first Egyptian or Syrian monks. Such a community would depend not so much on its organization, still less on its performance of a definite "work," as on the seriousness, the dedication and the spiritual strength of its members and on the authenticity of their vocation. Of course the group would have to be headed by an exceptional man, of deep spirituality and well grounded in monastic tradition.

It is significant that Rahner, who has laid such stress on the importance of the *person* in the diaspora situation (rather than the organized group) should cite St. Benedict as an example of one who admirably understood this kind of situation and adapted to it successfully. In all times of monastic crisis the monk instinctively looks back to the primitive simplicity of the origins, not in order to effect an archeological restoration of the past, but in order to see in what spirit renewal can be envisaged for the future. St. Benedict, Cassian, St. Basil, St. Pachomius, St. Anthony and St. Ammonas met the problems of their time in a spirit that is fully valid for our own, but we must emphasize the spirit and not the letter of their solutions.

The much publicized monastic revival of our own time suggests that the monastic life is, or can be, one of the ways in which the Church can adjust to her "diaspora situation." We might however mention that the monastic movement in its present state of progress does not give us evidence that perfect adjustment has been already achieved. The development of official monasticism in America so far, though certainly providential, has been in some ways more of a phenomenon than an achievement. In any case the vocational boom is over. The tidal wave has receded, and it has left stranded on the world's shores a great number of disillusioned aspirants who, for a few months or years, had desperately sought happiness and peace in the contemplative life. Their failure is to be blamed perhaps to some extent on them, but much more on the peculiar structural ambiguities of monasticism in its present condition. One may well doubt that monasticism can be expected to solve all the problems of the Church in the diaspora. This is not demanded of it. But let us hope that it can reach a creative solution of its own problems— and of this there seems to be some chance.

In any event the monastic revival continues unabated (though with less fanfare) and there can be no doubt that monasticism is now undergoing a more profound renewal than any that has been seen for eight hundred years—in other words, since the great ferment of the 11th and 12th centuries when the Carthusians, Camoldolese and Cistercians come into being and the Benedictines of Cluny spread all over Europe. Monastic problems and ideas are being rethought on the deepest level. The fundamental importance of such things as eremitical solitude is being rediscovered. The Biblical Movement is renewing monastic prayer and contemplation. Monks are trying to effect a liturgical renewal that will be relevant to their own way of life (and not just a "parish liturgy" for the monastic community).

The effectiveness of the monk's presence in the world and of his monastic witness to the Gospel of Christ will depend on his ability to see his own place in relation to the world correctly. He too must learn to understand his monastic calling in the general diaspora situation of the whole Church.

This is not going to be entirely easy, for while in theory, monks are supposed to think in terms of the original monastic ideals and the earliest sources, in practice they think, as they have been formed to think, in terms of an institution that preserves a set character, acquired in the days when the Church dominated all of society, and in which the monks played a most important part in helping her to do so.

Even though the *ordo monasticus* in western Europe was swept almost entirely out of existence by the French Revolution and the Napoleonic wars, it was restored in the nineteenth century by men whose devotion to the medieval past made it impossible for them to conceive a monastery that was not a fortress of medieval ideas, culture, worship and life. The whole concept of monastic revival was at first largely a matter of keeping alive in the world the values and customs that flouished in the Middle Ages, and which present an undeniably convincing picture of the vitality that once resulted from the Church's pervasive influence in feudal agrarian society.

There can be no question of the reality of these values. No one who has lived for ten or twenty years in a Cistercian or Benedictine monastery, or for that matter no one who has lived there even a few months, can deny that there is a basic sanity and order, a peace and sense of fulfillment, and authentic religious reality, that belong precisely to the ancient and medieval aspects of the monastic life. The fact that this authenticity exists, and that it makes possible a rare and balanced life in the midst of a convulsed and distracted world, certainly accounts for quite a few genuine monastic vocations. At the same time, it probably explains many of the failures and departures of vocations that were, perhaps, if the truth were known, equally genuine.

The unquestioned beauty and perennial significance of such things as Gregorian chant, the monastic ritual and habit, the Carolingian style of life maintained by the observances, the study of monastic texts and so on, are offset by the fact that many moderns are quite unable to live fruitful and "meaningful" lives in a milieu where *everything* is regulated according to the outlook and the habits of thought that once prevailed in a now extinct culture. Monastic obedience, for instance, is not simply the charismatic obedience that was envisaged by the monastic fathers and laid down in ancient Rules or in the Apothegmata of the desert. It is *also* heavily colored by the authoritarian world view of a later age in which the Church was a mighty temporal power and the monk regarded the world not only as the first Christians did (as something to be fled from) but also as the Medieval Church did (as a vast reservoir of secular power which could be harnessed for ecclesiastical use by commands and anathemas). The result is that monastic observance, poverty, obedience and so on tend tacitly to serve not only the purpose of the monk's own sanctification, but also the maintenance of an institution whose function is to proclaim the superiority of the feudal and hierarchical way of life as that which is fully and authentically "Christian" because it bears witness to the days when the Church enjoyed uncontested temporal power. Note, too, that the while modern monasticism goes back in its style and structure to the Carolingian monastic reform (the Cistercian return to Benedict was a not altogether successful attempt to get back beyond Charlemagne) it has also acquired numerous other features in course of time. Even the more austere orders do not retain the pure and severe nobility of the eleventh and twelfth century. There have been all the nuances and insinuations of late medieval piety, of Post-Tridentine organization and of ecclesiastical baroque, so that now the monastery is a highly complex organism where permanent and timeless values are confused with anachronisms and irrelevancies which are sometimes invested with all the solemnity of unchangeable dogma.

Much may still be said in favor of the order and beauty of this antique style of life, but, taken as a whole, it survives rather as an interesting anachronism than as an inspiration to the dormant religious sense that is still present in every man, no matter how "godless" he may claim to be. A monastery that simply offers an energetic and totally organized excursion into the past will not find much to recommend it in the diaspora as described by Karl Rahner.

It would be a very serious mistake to assume that the monastic order simply needs to be reshaped in a new contemporary mode, without a painstaking study of what is really essential to monasticism and what is not. There is no question that a thorough revision is called for in the accidentals of monastic observance, particularly in all those matters that affect the outward forms, the "style" of monastic life, work, obedience, silence, solitude, poverty and prayer. But any injury done to the essence of these things will cost dearly, and will threaten the existence of the monastery or Order that tries to dispense with what is indispensable.

Even in distinguishing substance and accident, we must remember that accidentals can have a serious importance of their own. Gregorian Chant, for example, is *accidental* in monastic liturgy. Yet it has a timelessness and universality, a true spiritual depth which makes it exceedingly difficult to replace by anything half as serious. Are we to assume that those who cling to Gregorian are merely antiquarian cranks? On the other hand, it is not always easy to use Gregorian Chant with English texts, and the vernacular liturgy is already well established in monasteries where the laybrothers have an English office. Perhaps the best solution would be the composition of simple new melodies in the Gregorian spirit but adapted to English texts.

An urgent need for new forms is now felt in monasteries everywhere. The danger in America is that the "new forms" will be instituted by men who have not had sufficient formation or experience in the living monastic tradition. These will be men who do not have a real sense of monastic values and who tend to consider all that is ancient to be ipso facto worthless and dead. While discarding irrelevances, they may at the same time throw out values that are irreplaceable. In this way, the monastic community will be reduced to a group of devout and organized cheesemakers (or schoolmasters), relatively prosperous, moderately disciplined, sharing the consolations of the latest liturgical piety and togetherness around the TV. If Rahner's predictions about the diaspora are correct, such communities will not be able to exist in it, and there will be no serious reason for them to do so. The argument that this style of life can be better appreciated by the men and world of our time has no weight, and in any case the monk should not concern himself directly with the impression he makes on his fellow man, even though he imagines that by projecting the "right image" he is exercising an indirect apostolate. The mere fact of consciously courting the esteem and appreciation of modern man immediately makes monasticism suspect (and rightly so) in his eyes.

Let us consider for a moment the man of our time, and let us assume that he is, by and large, already so indifferent to religion that he creates our diaspora situation for us. Whatever may be his state of indifference he may well know, intuitively, what to expect from a monastery. He may obscurely recognize that a monk is, or ought to be, a man who has gone through a radical experience of "conversion" or *metanoia* (even though these concepts may not be familiar). As a result of this response to a mysterious call, the monk has dedicated himself *unconditionally* to a radical quest for truth outside the bounds of social convention and organization, in a life of solitude.

In Christian tradition, the monastic life is an ascetic charism, or a special call of grace, demanding complete and unconditional renunciation of the ordinary style of human life, not in order to become part of a hierarchical institution with rigid rules and complex ceremonies, but in order to "seek God." (St. Benedict gives this sincere search for God, as the first sign of a true vocation.) What is important is the radical change and the unconditional dedication of the monk's life, and not its sacred formalities, its ceremonies and its hierarchical organization. The chief means used by the monk in his ardently committed and deeply personal "search" are silence, solitude, austerity, penance, poverty, obedience, meditation, reading, liturgical worship, productive work, chastity, and other characteristic disciplines. Where these are seriously pursued, whether in a systematically organized communal structure or out of it, the monastic charism may clearly manifest its presence even to one who has no idea of "charisms" or "vocations" or indeed of religion itself.

This charismatic vocation of the monk does, in

one sense, constitute a barrier between himself and the world. But we would show our total ignorance of the monastic life if we thought, by diminishing the seriousness of the vocation, to bring the monk into fruitful contact with the world. On the contrary, this separation from the world constitutes the basis, indeed the only valid basis, for his dialogue with the world. The monk, as such, is actually of no interest to anyone except in so far as he is really a monk. It would be a pity indeed for him to try to arouse sympathy and initiate serious conversations with "the world" by assuring everyone that he lives just as they do and shares all their interests without exception. Yet at the same time he must not insist so much on his difference that he withdraws into a resentful and negative solitude, completely turning his back on the rest of men, giving them up with their wickedness to justly deserved perdition. The monk who simply confronts the world of the diaspora with a polite curse, a formula of reprobation and disdain, or even a tear of genuine pity, will not justify his existence in it and will probably cease to exist.

What is really important is first of all a genuine renunciation of "the world," a fully authentic monastic solitude and a serious life of prayer, which alone can guarantee the truth and the charity of the monk's contact with the world. But then there is required a *fruitful sense of polarity* in

which the monk and, say, the atheist intellectual,
are able to discover not only that they can treat
one another politely, but that *they are indeed
brothers,* and that they share many of the same
concerns, for example in the area of world peace,
racial justice, and indeed everything that concerns
the well-being and development of man. This
"dialogue" will remain, in the life of the monk, a
secondary and accidental concern. The monastery
will by no means be organized *for* this as for an
end, even though secondary, since the monastic
charism is not "for" anything else. It is what it is:
the search for God in unconditional renunciation.
Yet if it paradoxically liberates the monk so that
he can, when occasion exceptionally demands,
communicate with his fellow man and indeed do
much to "give full scope to the forces of redemption" (Rahner) that must shape the world of his
time.

The monastic apostolate is, of course, primarily
one of prayer. But since some degree of hospitality
is one of the essentials of Benedictine life the monastic community does remain in contact with the
world, and should normally offer to men of the
world a place of silence, peace and retreat. The
need for such things in our world is now so serious
as to make this an obligation of charity for the
monk, but of course the monastery does not exist
in order to maintain a retreat house. The monk

may also accidentally exercise various other apostolic functions. The important thing however is for him not to become a prisoner of the routines and organization of an active life. He owes it to God, to the Church and to the world to preserve a certain monastic freedom so that his apostolic action, such as it is, will always retain a peaceful and charismatic character. It will be subject to the direct inspiration of the Holy Spirit and obedience in *particular* situations, not to organizational pressures and the demands of an exacting program. The diaspora situation may well make an organized apostolate of monks impossible in any case.

Many who have come face to face with this diaspora concept, as found in Rahner and in some Protestant theologians following Karl Barth, have been shocked by it and have felt that it was nothing but an expression of defeatism and withdrawal. In actual fact, it is intended to be quite the opposite. The "diaspora" is not the "ghetto." Rahner seems to feel that this new approach besides taking into account inescapable realities in the already existing situation not only of countries behind the iron curtain but also of other western European nations, allows for more spontaneous and more effective openness in the Christian apostolate. It is of course the kind of openness that was sought in the worker-priest movement, and is still sought and found by the Little Brothers founded by Charles de Foucauld.

From the monastic point of view, Protestant monasticism, which is one of the most original and important expressions of the monastic revival of the twentieth century, bears witness to this new combination of apostolic openness with authentic monachism. One thinks at once of Taizé, which is not absolutely typical in every respect: there are other less well known monastic and ecumenical communities which are even more free and which give less attention than Taizé to ancient and traditional forms.

3. MONASTIC THOUGHT IN THE RUSSIAN DIASPORA

It remains now to be said that this new "diaspora" outlook in monasticism has claimed attention for some time in Russian Orthodox thought. Of course the effect of the Soviet revolution on Russian monasticism was disastrous. The survival of monasticism in Russia (where in spite of ever increasing restrictions it is fully alive and exercises a definite spiritual influence) is almost miraculous. However, that is not the point. Russian monasticism is still trying to perpetuate not only the contemplative life but also the venerable cultural and liturgical forms characteristic of the pre-revolutionary Russian Church. The sense of "diaspora" must be sought elsewhere.

Modern Russian Orthodox writers who live literally in a "diaspora" (mostly in France) have carefully taken stock of the monastic movement and have traced the beginning of a new outlook back to the last century which was in fact the golden age of Russian monasticism. Léon Zander, regarding the monasticism of the Russian 19th century through the eyes of Dostoevski feels that the author of *The Brothers Karamazov* was speaking in some measure prophetically when he described the person and doctrine of the ideal *staretz* in Father Zossima. It is well known that Zossima is supposed to have been a life portrait of Staretz Ambrose of Optino or, as others seem to think, of St. Tikhon. Yet it is also known that the monks of Optino denied this and repudiated Zossima as a picture of their monastic ideal. What is the truth of the matter?

According to Léon Zander, the portrait of Zossima is not psychological or historical, but is a piece of "iconography." Zossima embodies and typifies not the 19th century monk but Dostoevski's own view of the inner meaning of monasticism. Indeed this Staretz is a "prophetic" type of what the monk of the future should be Zossima is, in other words, what Dostoevski thought the monks of the twentieth century needed to become. Now the curious thing about this is that Zossima is (as most of the Startzi also were beginning to be) a "diaspora" monk. In fact Zander quotes Rozanov and other writers who see in the clash between the Staretz, Zossima, and the fierce ascetic, Ferrapont, a contract between two forms of monasticism, the traditional and the "new." In fact, the Startzi were much criticized and attacked in their own time. They were by no means looked upon with unanimous favor in the monasteries. Their charismatic openness to the world, was reproved and they were criticized for the marginal life they tended to lead in relation to the traditional monastic framework. Ferrapont, as readers of *The Brothers Karamazov* will remember, is convinced that the Zossima is an impostor, a relaxed monk, undermining the ancient fabric of monasticism and playing ducks and drakes with the old ascetic traditions. In the contrast between these two characters, says Rozanov:

"Dostoevski has formulated an eternal truth, reaching down into the most essential reality (of monasticism). It is the truth of a conflict between two ideals: one which speaks a benediction and one which passes sentence of damnation, one which embraces the world and one which spits on the world, one which accepts pain (for itself) and one which plunges others deeper into pain."

Ferrapont stands for the full authority of the powerful and venerable monastic institution with all its medieval Byzantine traditions, all its hieratic observances, its sacred order, its security, its regularity, and its prestige. His ascesis is part of a mighty religious institution organized for power, manifesting that power in the inexorable condemnation of all that does not conform absolutely to its hieratic demands. It rejects as evil and damnable all that does not submit to the claims of a formidably organized body of traditions in thought, morality and worship. Hence whatever is not explicitly submissive becomes damnable, because it is part of the world of sin, and is opposed to the monastic city of God.

Zossima on the other hand is no ascetic, no ritualist, and his monastic practice is, by the standards of Ferrapont, lax and inconsistent. His observance (and that of the real Staretz Ambrose) is not austere and, what is worse, he is in free spontaneous communication with the wicked world, since sinners crowd to his cell for advice and blessing. Yet Zossima is in no sense merely an activist, on the contrary he is, according to Dostoevski, Rozanov, Zander, and modern Russian Orthodox writers, the "ikon of the true monk." He is truly solitary, fully dedicated and forgetful of self, a genuine man of God, totally converted to God yet perfectly aware of his own weakness and limitations, humble, merciful, and totally submissive not merely to law but to truth. Such monks (in the words of Zander) "preserve in their solitude the ikon of Christ, splendid and intact (since they are themselves that ikon), in all the purity of divine truth which has come down to us from the Fathers of the Church, the apostles and the martyrs. When the time is ripe, they will reveal this image to the shattered world . . ."

It is precisely this diaspora concept, which does not arrogate to the monastic order an official power which will infallibly bring a submissive world to the feet of Christ in His traditional and familiar aspect (the Christ painted on wood and covered with gold in the sanctuaries) but which hopes that the living Christ will reveal Himself in these meek ikons of flesh and blood, hidden in the world, solitary and humble men of prayer.

The monk of the diaspora is, then, the charismatic man of God, distinguished from the world only by his humility and his dedication, by his fidelity to life and to truth, rather than by his garments, the cloister in which he lives, by his hieratic gestures and ascetic practices. He does not live a strange life that makes him a wonder to the rest of men. In Dostoevski's novel we read that old Karamazov, the scoundrel and blasphemer, has nothing good to say to any of the monks except Zossima: but moved by the Staretz's simple words, he confesses: "Talking to you, one is able to breathe!"

The modern Russian theologians writing in the Paris diaspora are all keenly aware that this was a prophetic insight into the needs of our own time, for which they are now developing the idea of "monasticity of heart" (*monachisme interiorisé*). This is not merely a conventional notion of "an interior life for the layman" but the idea of the lay-monk, hidden solitary and unprotected, without the benefit of distinguishing marks and outward forms, called to deepen his monastic vocation "beneath the level of forms" and penetrating to the "ontological roots, the mystical essence" of the monastic life on an "ecumenical and trans-confessional level."*

In one word, we see here a perfect summary of the current intuitions of the monk's place in the diaspora world: a place in which he is most truly and perfectly himself, a *monachos,* a solitary and a man of prayer, poverty and labor, yet at the same time open to the world, and unhampered by the rigidities and frustrations of structures which still retain so many of the irrelevancies of the imperial

* The quotations from Zander and Rozanov are taken from an article by Léon Zander "Le Monaschime—réalité et idéal—dans l'oeuvre de Dostoievski" in *Le Millénaire du Mont Athos,* Chevetogne, 1963.

past. This is not to say that a sweeping and mindless modernization is called for to dispel all our troubles, or that great and valid traditions must now be thoughtlessly swept away. Still less does it mean that any form of irresponsibility can qualify as "adaptation" to new conditions.

However, if the monastic renewal is to be anything more than a pious wish, the monastic institution as we now know it must undergo significant changes. It must become less rigid, far more flexible than it is, much more capable of original and indeed charismatic initiatives. This is of course more a matter of special grace than of juridical reorganization, but even in our efforts to reorganize monastic structures, the true nature of the monastic vocation must be kept in mind above everything else.

In actual fact the real meaning of the monastic paradox of separation from the world and yet openness to it cannot be understood merely in terms of the classical interrelationship of action and contemplation. The monk is not simply a contemplative who "shares the fruits of his contemplation." He is one who is on pilgrimage "out of this world to the Father" and while remaining in the present life he is a sign of the world to come because his true perspectives are those of the eschatalogical Kingdom of God. Monks are "not of this world" as Christ is not of this world. (John 17:14–15)

Yet they participate in the crisis and tragedy of the world, which they see and understand quite differently from the world. Hence the concern of the monk can never be limited to the building up of an earthly and temporal structure, nor can he simply join in the labors and vicissitudes of the active apostolate.

The monk retains his own perspective and his own horizons which are those of the desert and of exile. But this in itself should enable him to have a special understanding of his fellow man in an age of alienation.

A TRIBUTE TO GANDHI

In 1931 Gandhi, who had been released from prison a few months before, came to London for a conference. The campaign of civil disobedience which had begun with the Salt March had recently ended. Now there were to be negotiations. He walked through the autumn fogs of London in clothes that were good for the tropics, not for England. He lived in the slums of London, coming from there to more noble buildings in which he conferred with statesmen. The English smiled at his bald head, his naked brown legs, the thin underpinnings of an old man who ate very little, who prayed. This was Asia, wise, disconcerting, in many ways unlovely, but determined upon some inscrutable project and probably very holy. Yet was it practical for statesmen to have conferences with a man reputed to be holy? What was the meaning of the fact that one could be holy, and fast, and pray, and be in jail, and be opposed to England all at the same time?

Gandhi thus confronted the England of the depression as a small, disquieting question mark. Everybody knew him, and many jokes were made about him. He was also respected. But respect implied neither agreement nor comprehension. It indicated nothing except that the man had gained public attention, and this was regarded as an achievement. Then, as now, no one particularly bothered to ask if the achievement signified something.

Yet I remember arguing about Gandhi in my school dormitory: chiefly against the football captain, then head prefect, who had come to turn out the flickering gaslight, and who stood with one hand in his pocket and a frown on his face that was not illuminated with understanding. I insisted that Gandhi was right, that India was, with perfect justice, demanding that the British withdraw peacefully and go home; that the millions of people who lived in India had a perfect right to run their own country. Such sentiments were of course beyond comprehension. How could Gandhi be right when he was *odd*? And how could I be right if I was on the side of someone who had the wrong kind of skin, and left altogether too much of it exposed?

A counter argument was offered but it was not an argument. It was a basic and sweeping assumption that the people of India were political and

moral infants, incapable of taking care of themselves, backward people, primitive, uncivilized, be-
nighted, pagan, who could not survive without
the English to do their thinking and planning
for them. The British Raj was, in fact, a purely
benevolent, civilizing enterprise for which the Indians were not suitably grateful . . .

Infuriated at the complacent idiocy of this
argument, I tried to sleep and failed.

Certain events have taken place since that
time. Within a dozen years after Gandhi's visit
to London there were more hideous barbarities
perpetuated in Europe, with greater violence and
more unmitigated fury than all that had ever been
attributed by the wildest imaginations to the des-
pots of Asia. The British Empire collapsed. India
attained selfrule. It did so peacefully and with dignity. Gandhi paid with his life for the ideals in
which he believed.

As one looks back over this period of confusion
and decline in the West, the cold war, and the
chaos and struggle of the world that was once
colonial, there is one political figure who stands
out from all the rest as an extraordinary leader of
men. He is radically different from the others.
Not that the others did not on occasion bear witness to the tradition of which they were proud
because it was Christian. They were often respectable, sometimes virtuous men, and many of them

were sincerely devout. Others were at least gen-
teel. Others, of course, were criminals. Judging
by their speeches, their programs, their expressed
motives were usually civilized. Yet the best that
could be said of them may be that they sometimes combined genuine capability and subjective
honesty. But apart from that they seemed to be
the powerless victims of a social dynamic that they
were able neither to control nor to understand.
They never seemed to dominate events, only to
rush breathlessly after the parade of cataclysms,
explaining why these had happened, and not
aware of how they themselves had helped precipi-
tate the worst of disasters. Thus with all their good
intentions, they were able at best to rescue themselves after plunging blindly in directions quite
other than those in which they claimed to be
going. In the name of peace, they wrought enormous violence and destruction. In the name of
liberty they exploited and enslaved. In the name
of man they engaged in genocide or tolerated it.
In the name of truth they systematically falsified
and perverted truth.

Gandhi on the other hand was dedicated to
peace, and though he was engaged in a bitter
struggle for national liberation, he achieved this
by peaceful means. He believed in serving the
truth by non-violence, and his non-violence was
effective in so far as it began first within himself.

It is certainly true that Gandhi was not above all criticism; no man is. But it is evident that he was unlike all the other world leaders of his time in that his life was marked by a wholeness and a wisdom, an integrity and a spiritual consistency that the others lacked, or manifested only in reverse, in consistent fidelity to a dynamism of evil and destruction. There may be limitations in Gandhi's thought, and his work has not borne all the fruit he himself would have hoped. These are factors which he himself sagely took into account, and having reckoned with them all, he continued to pursue the course he had chosen simply because he believed it to be true. His way was no secret: it was simply to follow conscience without regard for the consequences to himself, in the belief that this was demanded of him by God and that the results would be the work of God. Perhaps indeed for a long time these results would remain hidden as God's secret. But in the end the truth would manifest itself.

What has Gandhi to do with Christianity? Everyone knows that the Orient has venerated Christ and distrusted Christians since the first colonizers and missionaries came from the West. Western Christians often assume without much examination that this oriental respect for Christ is simply a vague, syncretistic and perhaps

romantic evasion of the challenge of the Gospel:
an attempt to absorb the Christian message into
the confusion and inertia which are thought to be
characteristic of Asia. The point does not need
to be argued here. Gandhi certainly spoke often
of Jesus, whom he had learned to know through
Tolstoy. And Gandhi knew the New Testament
thoroughly. Whether or not Gandhi "believed
in" Jesus in the sense that he had genuine Christian faith in the Gospel would be very difficult to
demonstrate, and it is not my business to prove it
or disprove it. I think that the effort to do so
would be irrelevant in any case. What is certainly
true is that Gandhi not only understood the ethic
of the Gospel as well, if not in some ways better,
than many Christians, but he is one of the very
few men of our time who applied Gospel principles to the problems of a political and social existence in such a way that his approach to these
problems was *inseparably* religious and political
at the same time.

He did this not because he thought that these
principles were novel and interesting, or because
they seemed expedient, or because of a compulsive
need to feel spiritually secure. The religious basis
of Gandhi's political action was not simply a program, in which politics were marshalled into the
service of faith, and brought to bear on the chari-
table objectives of a religious institution. For

Gandhi, strange as it may seem to us, political action had to be by its very nature "religious" in the sense that it had to be informed by principles of religious and philosophical wisdom. To separate religion and politics was in Gandhi's eyes "madness" because his politics rested on a thoroughly religious interpretation of reality, of life, and of man's place in the world. Gandhi's whole concept of man's relation to his own inner being and to the world of objects around him was informed by the contemplative heritage of Hinduism, together with the principles of Karma Yoga which blended, in his thought, with the ethic of the Synoptic Gospels and the Sermon on the Mount. In such a view, politics had to be understood in the context of service and worship in the ancient sense of *leitourgia* (liturgy, public work). Man's intervention in the active life of society was at the same time by its very nature *svadharma*, his own personal service (of God and man) and worship, *yajna*. Political action therefore was not a means to acquire security and strength for one's self and one's party, but a means of witnessing to the truth and the reality of the cosmic structure by making one's own proper contribution to the order willed by God. One could thus preserve one's integrity and peace, being detached from results (which are in the hands of God) and being free from the inner violence that comes from division and untruth, the usurpation of someone else's *dharma* in place of one's own *svadharma*. These perspectives lent Gandhi's politics their extraordinary spiritual force and religious realism.

The success with which Gandhi applied this spiritual force to political action makes him uniquely important in our age. More than that, it gives him a very special importance for Christians. Our attitude to politics tends to be abstract, divisive and often highly ambiguous. Political action is by definition secular and unspiritual. It has no really religious significance. Yet it is important to the Church as an institution in the world. It has therefore an *official* significance. We look to the Church to clarify principle and offer guidance, and in addition to that we are grateful if a Christian party of some sort comes to implement the program that has thus been outlined for us. This is all well and good. But Gandhi emphasized the importance of the individual person entering political action with a fully awakened and operative spiritual power in himself, the power of *Satyagraha,* non-violent dedication to truth, a religious and spiritual force, a wisdom born of fasting and prayer. This is the charismatic and personal force of the saints, and we must admit that we have tended to regard it with mistrust and unbelief, as though it were mere "enthusiasm" and "fanaticism." This is a lamentable mistake, because for one thing it tends to short circuit the power and light of grace, and it suggests that spiritual dedication is and must remain something entirely divorced from political action: something for the prie dieu, the sacristy or the study, but not for the marketplace. This in turn has estranged from the Church those whose idealism and generosity might have inspired a dedicated and creative intervention in political life. These have found refuge in groups dominated by a confused pseudo-spirituality, or by totalitarian messianism. Gandhi remains in our time as a sign of the genuine union of spiritual fervor and social action in the midst of a hundred pseudo-spiritual crypto-fascist, or communist movements in which the capacity for creative and spontaneous dedication is captured, debased and exploited by false prophets.

In a time where the unprincipled fabrication of lies and systematic violation of agreements has become a matter of course in power politics, Gandhi made this unconditional devotion to truth the mainspring of his social action. Once again, the radical difference between him and other leaders, even the most sincere and honest of them, becomes evident by the fact that Gandhi is chiefly concerned with truth and with service, *svadharma*, rather than with the possible success of his tactics upon other people, and paradoxically it was his religious conviction that made Gandhi a great politician rather than a mere tactician or operator. Note that *satyagraha* is matter for a vow, therefore of worship, adoration of the God of truth, so that his whole political structure is built on this and his other vows (*Ahimsa,* etc.) and becomes an entirely religious system. The vow of *satyagraha* is the vow to die rather than say what one does not mean.

The profound significance of *satyagraha* becomes apparent when one reflects that "truth" here implies much more than simply conforming one's words to one's inner thought. It is not by words only that we speak. Our aims, our plans of action, our outlook, out attitudes, our habitual response to the problems and challenges of life, "speak" of our inner being and reveal our fidelity or infidelity to ourselves. Our very existence, our life itself contains an implicit pretention to meaning, since all our free acts are implicit commitments, selections of "meanings" which we seem to find confronting us. Our very existence is "speech" interpreting reality. But the crisis of truth in the modern world comes from the bewildering complexity of the almost infinite contradictory propositions and claims to meaning uttered by millions of acts, movements, changes, decisions, attitudes, gestures, events, going on all around us. Most of all a crisis of truth is precipitated when men realize that almost all these claims are in fact without significance when they are not in great part entirely fraudulent.

Satyagraha for Gandhi meant first of all refusing to say "non-violence" and "peace" when one meant "violence" and "destruction." However, his wisdom differed from ours in this: he knew that in order to speak truth he must rectify more than his inner *intention*. It was not enough to say "love" and *intend* love thereafter proving the sincerity of one's own intentions by demonstrating the insincerity of one's adversary. "Meaning" is not a mental and subjective adjustment. For Gandhi, a whole lifetime of sacrifice was barely enough to demonstrate the sincerity with which he made a few simple claims: that he was not lying, that he did not intend to use violence or deceit against the English, that he did not think that peace and justice could be attained through violent or selfish means, that he did genuinely believe they could be assured by non-violence and self-sacrifice.

Gandhi's religio-political action was based on an ancient metaphysic of man, a philosophical wisdom which is common to Hinduism, Buddhism, Islam, Judaism, and Christianity: that "truth is the inner law of our being." Not that man is merely an abstract essence, and that our action must be based on logical fidelity to a certain definition of man. Gandhi's religious action is based on a religious intuition of *being* in man and in the world, and his vow of truth is a vow of fidelity to being in all its accessible dimensions. His wisdom is based on experience more than on logic. Hence the way of peace is the way of truth, of fidelity to wholeness and being, which implies a basic respect for life not as a concept, not as a sentimental figment of the imagination, but in its deepest most secret and most fontal reality. The first and fundamental truth is to be sought in respect for our own inmost being, and this in turn implies the recollectedness and the awareness which attune us to that silence in which alone Being speaks to us in all its simplicity.

Therefore Gandhi recognized, as no other world leader of our time has done, the necessity to be free from the pressures, the exorbitant and tyrannical demands of a society that is violent because it is essentially greedy, lustful and cruel. Therefore he fasted, observed days of silence, lived frequently in retreat, knew the value of solitude, as well as of the totally generous expenditure of his time and energy in listening to others and communicating with them. He recognized the impossibility of being a peaceful and nonviolent man if one submits passively to the insatiable requirements of a society maddened by overstimulation and obsessed with the demons of noise, voyeurism and speed.

"Jesus died in vain," said Gandhi, "if he did not teach us to regulate the whole of life by the eternal law of love." Strange that he should use this expression. It seems to imply at once concern and accusation. As Asians sometimes do, Gandhi did not hesitate to confront Christendom with the principles of Christ. Not that he judged Christianity, but he suggested that the professedly Christian civilization of the west was in fact judging itself by its own acts and its own fruits. There are certain Christian and humanitarian elements in democracy, and if they are absent, democracy finds itself on trial, weighed in the balance, and no amount of verbal protestations can prevent it from being found wanting. Events themselves will procede inexorably to their conclusion. *Pacem in Terris* has suggested the same themes to the meditation of modern Europe, American and Russia. "Civilization" must learn to prove its claims by a capacity for the peaceful and honest settlement of disputes, by genuine concern for justice toward people who have been shamelessly exploited and races that have been systematically oppressed, or the historical preeminence of the existing powers will be snatched from them by violence, perhaps in a disaster of cosmic proportions.

Gandhi believed that the central problem of our time was the acceptance or the rejection of a basic law of love and truth which had been made known to the world in traditional religions and most clearly by Jesus Christ. Gandhi himself expressly and very clearly declared himself an adherent of this one law. His whole life, his political action, finally even his death, were nothing but a witness to his commitment. "IF LOVE IS NOT THE LAW OF OUR BEING THE WHOLE OF MY ARGUMENT FALLS TO PIECES."

What remains to be said? It is true that Gandhi expressly dissassociated himself from Christianity in any of its visible and institutional forms. But it is also true that he built his whole life and all his activity upon what he conceived to be the law of Christ. In fact, he died for this law which was at the heart of his belief. Gandhi was indisputably sincere and right in his moral commitment to the law of love and truth. A Christian can do nothing greater than follow his own conscience with a fidelity comparable to that which Gandhi obeyed what he believed to be the voice of God. Gandhi is, it seems to me, a model of integrity whom we cannot afford to ignore, and the one basic duty we all owe to the world of our time is to imitate him in "disassociating ourselves from evil in total disregard of the consequences."

PART THREE

Letters in a Time of Crisis

LETTERS IN A TIME OF CRISIS

1. TO A PAPAL VOLUNTEER

This morning I said Mass for you and will do the same Passion Sunday, (tomorrow) and Monday and then I will offer a couple more masses later on before Easter. May God bless your decision to go to Brazil as Papal Volunteers. You ask for some suggestions. I am no authority on the subject, but here are one or two notions which occur to me.

You do not need to be told that your work will not be easy. Also it will probably not be rewarding. Therefore from the very first you must be extremely realistic about the expectations of a human "reward." You must learn to mistrust even unconscious expectations, which may in fact be of a kind to wreak havoc with you.

I think perhaps the first thing you will discover is that North Americans are not always popular, and your very motives may be suspected from the first, by many. Certainly there will be people who

237

will maliciously discredit you. Others will take everything for granted and perhaps not give you any thanks. Yet at the same time it is important that you patiently work for a real solid rapport on the human level, because this will give a meaningful and genuinely Christian dimension to your efforts.

My advice to you is to go much slower than you are evidently preparing to do. Spend several months in Brazil getting to know people on your own level before you start in the tenements. You should go to Rio and Sao Paolo first, and spend a good long time in each place getting to know Brazil and its problems, not in sociology courses but in conversations with people who know what is going on. I recommend first of all that you get to know the Benedictines in Rio, and they in turn will get you in contact with Benedictines in the north. But you should know Rio and Sao Paolo, even if that is not what you will find in Bahia. Take your time, get to know what is what, and above all, for heaven's sake, adjust that American image. We of the U.S. have unfortunately placed too much trust in our mass media and we have the most fabulously unreal image of ourselves. We are living in illusion. We have no concept of how we look to other people, and we do not know how to swallow their exaggerations about us, which go the other extreme. Nor can we get them to respond to

a reality in ourselves which we are passionately engaged in hiding, without realizing it.

One of the first things will be also to break
through the unreal notions we have fabricated for
ourselves about Latin Americans. These are complex and often very wonderful people. The Brazil-
ians have a great warmth, merriment and kind-
ness. They are less embittered than some of the
other Latin Americans, so far. They will respect
you if you have a little sophistication and reserve
and much humor. Don't sulk with them. Laugh
off the inevitable problems, and *be ready to tolerate
all kinds of delays.* They are not obsessed with
efficiency and practicality, and may seem madden-
ingly irresponsible. Take your time and expect
them to take theirs. *Be very tolerant.* Be as unde-
manding as you can. This slow tempo will help
the contemplative side of your life: but if you get
in a frenzy and want quick results, you will run
into spiritual disaster. I repeat, disaster.

You will have to give up the passion for results
from the start, and you must help the people
simply for the love of it. Don't push for results or
for rewards. Don't demand appreciation, even unconsciously (if possible). Appreciate *them.* If you
do, you may never come back here, you may live
there happily ever after. Worse things could happen!

One thing: recognize the fact that your presence and activity may well seem to be an implied reproach to the Brazilian medical profession, or to the Brazilian social workers, Church, etc. etc. That is one of the chief reasons for not doing anything fast. Do not rush in with the implication that you are going in five weeks to wake them all up and make them recognize the superiority and benevolence of the USA. This is harming Papal Volunteers, Peace Corps Workers, and other people, as well as our national reputation, in all kinds of ways and places.

Recognize too that you may have a great deal to learn from the people of Brazil. If you go there with the idea that you are going to give, with great magnanimity, and without any awareness of your need for them, then you will fail. If God is calling you there, it may be more because you need Brazil than because Brazil needs you. I say this in all frankness and sobriety.

Finally, the children. I don't know if you have a strict right to take them into the slums of Bahia. Perhaps the best thing would be to find a school (again here the Benedictines will help) where they could board or be taken care of.

There is a great deal more I could say: you must preserve a leisurely and contemplative approach in all this. It is going to be a hot climate, and you will have to go slow, and sleep after dinner, and all that sort of thing. Prolong the siesta perhaps with a little reading and meditation. You can readily give a contemplative character to the tempo of the Brazilian life if you want to, but if you insist in U.S. standards and tempo you can kiss the contemplative life goodbye there, you will be in conflict with everybody beginning with yourself.

Finally don't demand too much of yourself to begin with: and don't be surprised if in this new situation some unlovely aspects of your own character begin to appear. Don't run away from them, but be patient and quiet and trust God. Thank Him for everything. He is working in your heart now, and will continue.

As to Communism: better listen to what they are saying so as to know what their arguments are, in order to refute them by your lives. The knowledge of Communism that prevails in America is mostly legend and myth, and actually gives the Reds credit for being much more demonically intelligent than they actually are. You need to know the reality about them which is complex and vulnerable in many ways. The strongest stand to take is to have a knowledge of how they have in actual fact long ago swung into a position of complete contradiction to Marx and got rid of all his most telling ideas, in order to substitute a kind of dogmatic and artificial structure that is opposed to what he really taught. If you know this you can understand and handle them better.

2. TO ALCEU AMOROSO LIMA

It was a great pleasure to receive your letter, and above all, do not apologize for writing to me in Portuguese. I enjoy very much reading it, though it would probably be impossible for me to write it very coherently. It is a language I delight in, warm and glowing, one of the most human of tongues, richly expressive and in its own way innocent. Perhaps I say this speaking subjectively, not having read all that may have enlightened me in some other sense. But it seems to me that Portuguese has never yet been used for such barbarities as German, English, French or Spanish. And I love the Brazilian people. I keep wanting to translate Jorge de Lima. I have the poems of Manuel Bandeira and Carlos Drummond de Andrade and several others. I like them and read them all.

Now as to the topic of your letter. I believe it is very important that we exchange ideas from time to time. This is a crucial and perhaps calamitous moment in history, a moment in which reason and understanding threaten to be swallowed up, even if man himself manages to survive. It is all very well for me to meditate on these things in the shelter of the monastery: but there are times when this shelter itself is deceptive. Everything is deceptive today. And grains of error planted innocently in a well kept greenhouse can become gigantic, deadly trees.

Everything healthy, everything certain, everything holy: if we can find such things, they all need to be emphasized and articulated. For this it is necessary that there be a genuine and deep communication between the hearts and minds of men, communication and not the noise of slogans or the repetition of clichés. Genuine communication is becoming more and more difficult, and when speech is in danger of perishing or being perverted in the amplified noise of beasts, perhaps it becomes obligatory for a monk to try to speak. There is therefore it seems to me every reason why we should attempt to cry out to one another and comfort one another, in so far as this may be possible, with the truth of Christ and also with the truth of humanism and reason. For faith cannot be preserved if reason goes under, and the Church cannot survive if man is destroyed: that is to say if his humanity is utterly debased and mechanized, while he himself remains on earth as the instrument of enormous and unidentified forces like those which press us inexorably to the brink of nuclear war.

Yes, we should try to understand Castro together. This is a significant and portentous phenomenon, and it has many aspects. Not the least, of course, is the fact that Castro is now about to become a figure with a hundred heads all over Latin America. One aspect of it that I can see is the embitterment and disillusionment of this well-intentioned man who was weak and passionate and easily abused. The man who like all of us wanted to find a third way, and was immediately swallowed up by one of the two giants that stand over all of us. The United States could have helped him and could perhaps have saved him: but missed its chance.

It is indeed supremely necessary for us to try to think together a little of the Church in the Americas. This is an enormous obligation. There is much activity but not so much thought, and in any case the activity may have come late. I do not know what I can contribute, but the issue has been close to my heart for several years.

We are all nearing the end of our work. The night is falling upon us, and we find ourselves without the serenity and fulfillment that were the lot of our fathers. I do not think this is necessarily a sign that anything is lacking, but rather is to be taken as a greater incentive to trust more fully in the mercy of God, and to advance further into His mystery. Our faith can no longer serve merely as a happiness pill. It has to be the Cross and the Resurrection of Christ. And this it will be, for all of us who so desire.

3. TO A PROFESSOR OF
   HUMANITIES

I have taken a little time to get around to your letter about your Program for Christian Culture. This is a very important question and I am afraid I will not entirely do justice to it, but at least I can set down a few thoughts that occur to me, and hope for the best.

First of all, the urgent need for Christian Humanism. I stress the word humanism, perhaps running the risk of creating wrong impressions. What is important is the fully Christian notion of man: a notion radically modified by the mystery of the Incarnation. This I think is the very heart of the matter. And therefore it seems to me that a program of Christian culture needs to be rooted in the biblical notion of man as the object of divine mercy, and of special concern on the part of God, as the spouse of God, as, in some mysterious sense, an epiphany of the divine wisdom. Man in Christ. The New Adam, presupposing the Old Adam, presupposing the old paradise and the new paradise, the creation and the new creation.

At the present time man has ceased to be seen as any of these. The whole Christian notion of man has been turned inside out, instead of paradise we have Auschwitz. But note that the men who went into the ovens at Auschwitz were still the same elect race, the object of the divine predilection . . . These perspectives are shattering, and they are vital for Christian culture. For then in the study of Europe and European Christianity, Latin Christianity, we come up against a dialectic of fidelity and betrayal, understanding and blindness. That we have come to a certain kind of "end" of the development of western Christian society is no accident, nor yet is it the responsibility of Christian culture, for Christian culture has precisely saved all that could be saved. Yet was this enough?

These are terrible problems and I am sure no one can answer. In a word, perhaps we might profitably run the risk, not just of assuming that Christian culture is a body of perfections to be salvaged but of asking where there was infidelity and imperfection. And yet at the same time stressing above all the value and the supreme importance of our western Christian cultural heritage. For it is the survival of religion as an abstract formality without a humanist matrix, religion apart from man and almost in some sense apart from God Himself (God figuring only as a Lawgiver and not as a Savior) religion without any human epiphany in art, in work, in social forms: this is what is killing religion in our midst today, not the atheists. So that one who seeks God without culture and without humanism tends inevitably to promote a religion that is irreligious and even unconsciously atheistic, because it is first of all abstract and anti-human.

It would seem that the a-cultural philistinism of our society were the preferred instrument of demonic forces to finally eviscerate all that is left of Christian humanism. I am thinking of an appalling item read in our refectory yesterday in which we were informed that at last religion was going to be put on the map in America by the "advertising industry" (*sic*). Here with a sublimely cynical complacency we were informed that now everybody would be urged in the most shallow importunate, tasteless and meaningless ways, that they had to go to a Church or Synagogue or conventicle of some sect. Just get into the nearest conventicle as fast as your legs can carry you, brother, and get on your knees and *worship;* we don't give a hoot how you do it or why you do it, but you've got to get in there and worship, brother, because the advertising industry says so and it is written right on the napkin in the place where you eat your fallout lettuce sandwich.

Sorry if I sound like a beatnik, but this is what is driving intelligent people as far from Christianity as they can travel. Hence in one word a pretended Christianity without the human and cultural dimensions which nature herself has provided, in history, in social tradition etc., our religion becomes a lunar landscape of meaningless gestures and observances. A false supernaturalism which theoretically admits that grace builds on nature and then proceeds to eliminate everything natural: there you have the result of forgetting our cultural and humanistic tradition!

To my mind it is very important that this experiment is being conducted in a Catholic women's college. This is to me a hopeful sign. I think women are perhaps capable of salvaging something of humanity in our world today. Certainly they have a better chance of grasping and understanding and preserving a sense of Christian culture. And of course I think the wisdom of Sister Madeleva has a lot to do with the effectiveness of this experiment and its future possibilities. The word *wisdom* is another key word, I suspect. We are concerned not just with culture but also with wisdom, above all.

Here I might mention someone who I think ought to be known and consulted as a *choregos* for our music, and that is Clement of Alexandria. In fact I think one might profitably concentrate a great deal of attention on the Alexandrian school, not only the Christians, but all that extraordinary complex of trends, the Jewish and the Gnostic and neoplatonist, Philo above all, and then the desert Fathers too, just outside. And Origen. And the

Palestinians who reacted against Alexandria, and the Antiocheans. Here we have a crucially important seed bed of future developments.

But the whole question of Christian culture is a matter of wisdom more than of culture. For wisdom is the full epiphany of God the Logos, in man and the world of which man is a little exemplar. Wisdom does not reveal herself until man is seen as microcosm, and the whole world is seen in relation to the measure of man. It is this measure which is essential to Christian culture, and whatever we say or read it must always be remembered. I could develop this more, but have no time. I could refer you to a booklet that is being printed in a limited edition by Victor Hammer, on this. I will ask him if perhaps he would consent to send the college a copy. If there is no end of money to spend on books, perhaps the library would want to buy it from him, as he only prints editions of fifty or sixty and makes his living on the proceeds.

Mark Van Doren was here talking about liberal education recently. He would be a good man to consult. He stresses the point that liberal education is that which frees an (adult) mind from the automatisms and compulsions of a sensual outlook. Here again we rejoin the Alexandrians and Greeks. The purpose of a Christian humanism should be to liberate man from the mere status of *animalis homo* (*sarkikos*) to at least the level of *rationalis*

(*psychicos*)and better still, spiritual, or pneu-
matic. The spiritual man is fully man precisely
because he has fulfilled his latent potentialities by
life "in the Spirit" i.e. the Holy Spirit, the Spirit
of Christ.

4. TO A STATESMAN'S WIFE

It seems to me that the great problem we face
is not Russia but war itself. War is the main enemy
and we are not going to fully make sense unless we
see that. Unless we fight war, both in ourselves
and in the Russians, and wherever else it may be,
we are purely and simply going to be wrecked by
the forces that are in us. The great illusion is to
assume that we are perfectly innocent, peace-lov-
ing and right while the Communists are devils in-
carnate. I admit they are no angels and they have
been guilty of some frightful crimes against humanity. Soviet power is without doubt a terrible
menace, to the safety of the human race. I admit
also that we must not go to the extreme of con-
demning ourselves without reason. We have made
mistakes and will make more of them, but I hope
we can learn to be a bit more realistic about all
that, as long as we avoid the biggest mistake of all:
plunging the world into nuclear war by any de-
liberate decision of our own. I think also it is tre-

mendously important for us to work out a collabo-
rative control scheme with the USSR to check on
various possible accidents that might trigger a nuclear war.

Why is war such a problem to us? I do not pretend to be able to give a reason for everything
under the sun, but if I am to be consistent with my
own experience and my religious beliefs, as well as
with the crying evidence that is all around us, one
main reason is our moral decline. As a nation we
have begun to float off into a moral void and all the
sermons of all the priests in the country (if they
preach at all) are not going to help much. We
have got to the point where the promulgation of
any kind of moral standard automatically releases
an anti-moral response in a whole lot of people. It
is not with them above all that I am concerned, but
with the "good" people, the right thinking people, who stick to principle all right except where it
conflicts with the chance to make money. It seems
to me that there are very dangerous ambiguities
about our democracy in its actual present condition. I wonder to what extent our ideals are now a
front for organized selfishness and systematic irresponsibility. The shelter business certainly brought
out the fact that some Americans are not too far
from the law of the jungle. If our affluent society
ever breaks down and the façade is taken away,
what are we going to have left? Suppose we *do*

have a war, and fifty million people are left to tell the tale: what kind of people are they going to be? What kind of a life will they live? By what standards? We cannot go on living every man for himself. The most actual danger of all is that we may some day float without realizing it into a nice tight fascist society in which all the resentments and all the guilt in all the messed up teen-agers (and older ones) will be channeled in a destructive groove.

We are living in a dream world. We do not know ourselves or our adversaries. We are myths to ourselves and they are myths to us. And we are secretly persuaded that we can shoot it out like the sheriffs and cattle rustlers on TV. This is not reality and the President can do a tremendous amount to get people to see the fact, more than any single person. If he can get the country to face reality and accept it and try to cope with it on a sober basis, without expecting miracles at every turn, we may begin to get ourselves together. But for this one has to have motives and principles, and that is just what too many people have thrown overboard.

I personally wish the Church in America and everywhere were more articulate and definite about nuclear war. Statements of Pius XII* have left us some terribly clear principles about this. We can-

* This was written before *Pacem in Terris*.

not go on indefinitely relying on the kind of provisional framework of a balance of terror. If as Christians we were more certain of our duty, it might put us in a very tight spot politically but it would also merit for us special graces from God, and these we need badly.

5. TO DOROTHY DAY

I have read your latest "On Pilgrimage" in the December *Catholic Worker,* and I want to say how good I think it is. In many ways I think it is about the best thing I have seen that came out of this whole sorry shelter business. What you say in the beginning is clear and incontrovertible. You make one unanswerable point after another, though I don't claim that people are not going to answer you and some may get quite hot about the fact that you want to point out that Castro may have had good intentions and in actual fact have been less wicked than our mass media want him to have been. People who are scared and upset use a very simple logic, and they think that if you defend Castro as a human being you are defending all the crimes that have ever been committed by Communism anywhere, and they feel that you are threatening them.

But as Christians we have to keep on insisting

on the distinction between the man, the person, and the actions and policies attributed to him and his group. We have to remember the terrible danger of projecting on to others all the evil we find in ourselves, so that we justify our own hatred and destructiveness by directing them against a projected evil.

The basic thing in Christian ethics is to look at the *person* and not at the *nature*. That is why natural law so easily degenerates, in practice and in casuistry, to jungle law which is no law at all. Because when we consider "nature" we consider the general, the theoretical, and forget the concrete, the individual, the personal reality of the one confronting us. Hence we can see him not as our other self, not as Christ, but as our demon, our evil beast, our nightmare. This, I am afraid, is what a wrong, unintelligent and unchristian emphasis on natural law has done.

Persons are known not by the intellect alone, not by principles alone, but only by love. It is when we love the other, the enemy, that we obtain from God the key to an understanding of who he is, and who we are. It is only this realization that can open to us the real nature of our duty, and of right action.

To *shut out* the person and to refuse to consider him as a person, as an other self, we resort to the impersonal "law" and "nature." That is to say we block off the reality of the other, we cut the intercommunication of our nature and his nature, and we consider only our own nature with its rights, its claims, its demands. In effect, however, we are considering *our nature in the concrete* and *his nature in the abstract.* And we justify the evil we do to our brother because he is no longer a brother, he is merely an adversary, an accused, an evil being.

To restore communication, to see our oneness of nature with him, and to respect his personal rights, his integrity, his worthiness of love, we have to see ourselves as accused along with him, condemned to death along with him, sinking into the abyss with him, and needing, with him, the ineffable gift of grace and mercy to be saved. Then instead of pushing him down, trying to climb out by using his head as a stepping stone for ourselves, we help ourselves to rise by helping him to rise. When we extend our hand to the enemy who is sinking in the abyss, God reaches out for both of us, for it is He first of all who extends our hand to the enemy. It is He who "saves himself" in the enemy who makes use of us to recover the lost groat which is His image in our enemy.

It is all too true that when many theologians talk about natural law, they are talking about jungle law. And this is not law at all. It is not natural either. The jungle law is not natural. Or rather, perhaps the true primeval life is natural in a higher sense than we realize. The "jungles" which are our cities are worse than jungles, they are sub-jungles, and their law is a sub-jungle law, a sub-sub natural law. And here I refer not to those who are considered the lowest in society, but rather those who exercise power in the jungle city, and use it unscrupulously and inhumanly, whether on the side of "law and order" or against law and order.

And yet, as a priest and as one obligated by my state to preach and explain the truth, I cannot take occasion from this abusive view of natural law to reject the concept altogether. On the contrary, if I contemn and reject *en bloc* all the ethical principles which appeal to the natural law, I am in fact undercutting the Gospel ethic at the same time. It is customary to go through the Sermon on the Mount and remark on the way it appears *to contrast with* the mosaic law and the natural law. On the contrary, it seems to me that the Sermon on the Mount is not only a supernatural fulfilment of the natural law, but an affirmation of "nature" in the true, original Christian meaning: of nature assumed by Christ in the Incarnation. As a remote basis for this, we might consider Colossians 1:9–29, noting especially that we humans who were at enmity with one another are "reconciled in the body of His flesh." Christ

the Lord is the Word Who has assumed our
nature, which is one in all of us.

He has perfectly fulfilled and so to speak trans-
figured and elevated not only the nature and the
natural law which is, in its most basic expression,
treating our brother as one who has the same
nature as we have. Now here is the point where
our ethical speculation has gone off the rails. In
the biblical context, in the context of all spiritual
and ancient religions that saw this kind of truth,
the good which man must do and the evil he must
avoid according to the natural law must be based
on an experience or a realization of connaturality
with our brother.

Example: if I am in a fallout shelter and trying
to save my life, I must see that the neighbor who
wants to come in to the shelter also wants to save
his life as I do. I must experience his need and his
fear just as if it were my need and my fear. This
is not supernatural at all, it is purely and simply
the basis of the natural law, which of course has
been elevated and supernaturalized. But it is *per se*
natural. If then I experience my neighbor's need
as my own, I will act accordingly, and if I am
strong enough to act out of love, I will cede my
place in the shelter to him. This I think is possible,
at least theoretically, even on the basis of natural
love. In fact personally I am sure it is. But at the

same time there is the plentiful grace of God to enable us to do this.

Now, to approach casuistry: if the person who threatens the life of my children, say, is raving mad: I have a duty to protect my children, it may be necessary to restrain the berserk guy by force . . . etc. But my stomach revolts at the casuistical approach to a question like this at a time like this.

My point is this, rather, that I don't think we ought to simply discard the concept of the natural law as irrelevant. On the contrary I think it is very relevant once it is properly understood. Matthew 5:21–26 is, to my way of thinking, a vindication of human nature because it is a *restoration* of human nature. I admit that this view of nature is perhaps not that of the scholastics but rather that of the Greek Fathers. But it is to my way of thinking more natural, more in accord with the nature of man, to be nonviolent, to be not even angry with his brother, not to say "raca" etc. However we cannot recover this fulness of nature without the grace of God.

In this peculiar view, then, the natural law is not merely what is ethically right and fitting for fallen man considered purely in his fallen state: it is the law of his nature as it came to him from the hand of God, the law imprinted in his nature by the image of God. Every man is made by his very *nature,* in the image of God. Hence the natural law is the law which inclines our inmost heart to conform to the image of God which is in the deepest center of our being, and it also inclines our hearts to respect and love our neighbor as the image of God. However this concept of nature is only comprehensible when we see that it presupposes grace and calls for grace and as it were sighs and groans for grace. Actually our contradictions within ourselves make us realize that without grace we are lost.

In a word, then, I want with my whole heart to fulfil in myself this natural law, in order to fulfil also the law of grace to which it leads me. And I want with my whole heart to realize and fulfil my communion of nature with my brother, in order that I may be by that very fact one with him in Christ. But here, as I said in the beginning, I must rise above nature, I must *see the person* (this is still possible to nature "alone") and I must see the person in Christ, in the spirit.

6. TO EDWARD DEMING
    ANDREWS

Forgive please this very long delay in thanking you for the copy of *Shaker Furniture* which will remain a valued possession in our novitiate library.

I believe it is of the greatest importance for the novices to see these things, and get used to this wonderful simplicity. This wordless simplicity, in which the works of quiet and holy people speak humbly for themselves. How important that is in our day when we are flooded with a tidal wave of meaningless words: and worse still when in the void of those words the sinister power of hatred and destruction is at work. The Shakers remain as witnesses to the fact that only humility keeps man in communion with truth, and first of all with his own inner truth. This one must know without knowing it, as they did. For as soon as a man becomes too self-consciously aware of "his truth" he lets go of it and embraces an illusion.

I am so glad you liked the translation of Clement of Alexandria. If it ever gets printed, I will gladly send you a copy. New Directions is not in a hurry to decide because we are working on a more urgent project.

Speaking of Clement and Alexandria, do you know of Philo Judaeus, the Jewish Platonist who flourished in that city? He has a very intriguing book *De Therapeutis* (which I have not yet found and read). In this book he speaks of Jewish monastic communities in Egypt in which there are some similarities with the Shakers. Particularly the fact that they were contemplative communities of men and women, living separately and joining in worship, though "segregated." It would seem there might be many interesting facts in this book, and I recommend it to your curiosity. Alexandria remains a fascinating place, and I am sure that more study of the intellectual and spiritual movements that flourished there will prove very rewarding.

7. A LETTER ON
''DISINTERESTED LOVE''

What I said about the disinterested love of God represented my interest, at that time, in the medieval Platonic tradition, running through St. Augustine and Duns Scotus, and including the Cistercian monks. A monastery is supposed to be a "school of charity" (i.e. disinterested love). A school of *agape* rather than *eros*. Disinterested love is also called the "love of friendship," that is to say a love which rests in the good of the beloved, not in one's own interest or satisfaction, not in one's own pleasure. A love which does not exploit, manipulate, even by "serving," but which simply "loves." A love which, in the words of St. Bernard, "loves because it loves" and for no other reason or purpose, and is therefore "perfectly free." This is a spiritual ideal which also had secular counterparts in the courtly love of the

Provençal poets, and there is a whole interesting literary tradition, which finally gets lost in the sand.

The ideal of disinterested love is one that in one form or other crops up in all mystical religion. It is, in a very intellectual form, found in the off-print on Zen which I sent you. It is found in a wonderfully rich and charming human expression in the mysticism of the hassidin, Jewish tzaddiks of Poland and Central Europe.

The way I would express it now, is in purely religious and symbolic terms. That we should "love God" not merely to convince ourselves that we are good people, or to get a warm glow of peace, or to fit in with an approving group, or to get rid of anxiety, but to throw all that to the winds, and anxiety or not, even though we realize the utter abyss of our inadequacy, to realize that this simply does not matter in the "eyes of God" for, as we are, with our misfortunes and needs, "we are His joy" and He delights to be loved by us with perfect confidence in Him because He is love itself. This is of course not capable of being put in scientific language, it is religious symbol, or if you prefer, "myth." But if you will be patient with it, and stay with it, I think you will find it is the most fundamental symbol and the deepest truth: at least I am trying to express that which is deepest and most essential. My own symbol may be very poor. But that is the way I would put it. It is not that we have to sweat and groan to placate an austere Father God in our own imagination, but rather to realize, with liberation and joy, that *He is not that at all.* That in fact He is none of our idols, none of our figments, nothing that we can imagine anyway, but that He is Love Itself. And if we realize this and love Him simply and purely in order to "please Him," we become as it were His "crown" and His "delight" and life itself is transformed in this light which is disinterested love.

Freud did not think much of a mysticism which was described as "an oceanic feeling" and I think in a way he was rather right in his suspicion of it, though he was a great old puritan that man! Oceanic feeling is not something that has to be rejected just because it might suggest a danger of narcissism. But pure love, disinterested love, is far beyond the reach of narcissism and I think even old Freud would have caught on that this was an equivalent of mature and oblative love in the ordinary psychophysical sphere.

I hope these few words from me will be of some help. The rest may be found perhaps in the off-print. Suzuki is an interesting and splendid mind, and a great Buddhist. And I enjoyed trying to keep up with his Zen, which after all does have some parallel in the western tradition. Disinterested love opens a way to the understanding of both.

8.   TO ROBERT LAX

I have before me your exceedingly ribald Christmas card in many foreign languages inciting to joy.

Here without feet running in the sand or on the burning deck beneath the whips here amid the wolves we meditate on *joyeux noel*.

Here with the ship of state already half submerged and with waters up to our beard standing nobly on the tottering captain's bridge,

We Santa Claus salute you.

9.   NEW YEAR, 1962

It has been a marvelous Christmas for me. The darkest in my life and yet in many ways the clearest and most radiant. Dark of course because of the situation we are all in. And radiant because one comes to understand that the darkness is there for a reason also. That the Light has come into darkness which has not understood it: this we have known long since. But we have not known all the implications. Nor have we understood the immense depth of the mystery which we nevertheless know by rote: that the Light not only shall and will triumph over the darkness, but already has. This is not a spiritual bromide, it is the heart of our Christian faith. Have you ever read the English mystic Julian (sometimes wrongly called Juliana) of Norwich? I will write to you about her some time. She is a mighty theologian, in all her simplicity and love.

Though "all manner of things shall be well," we cannot help but be aware, on the threshold of 1962 that we have enormous responsibilities and tasks of which we are perhaps no longer capable. Our sudden, unbalanced top-heavy rush into technological mastery has left us without the spiritual means to face our problems. Or rather, we have thrown the spiritual means away. Even the religious people have not been aware of the situation, not become aware until perhaps too late. And here we all stand as prisoners of our own scientific virtuosity, ruled by immense power that we ought to be ruling and cannot. Our weapons dictate what we are to do. They force us into corners. They give us our living, they sustain our economy, they bolster up our politicians, they sell our mass media, in short we live by them. But if they continue to rule us we will also most surely die by them. For they have now made it plain that they are the friends of the "preemptive first strike." They are most advantageous to those who use them first. And consequently nobody wants to be found dead using them second. Hence the weapons keep us in a state of fury and desperation, with our fingers poised over the button and our eyes glued on the radar screen. You know what happens when you keep your eye fixed on something. You begin to see things that aren't there. It is very possible that in 1962 the weapons will tell someone that there has been enough waiting, and he will obey, and we will all have had it.

It shows what comes of believing in science more than in God. The business about Pharaoh in Exodus is not so far out after all, is it? Bricks without straw, and more than that. Faith is the principle of the only real freedom we have. Yet history is full of the paradox that the liberation of the mind of man by Christianity did a great deal to make the development of science possible too. Yet you can't blame all this on the Bible or on the Greeks or on the Council of Nicea (which brought into the spotlight the meaning of the Person). There was also too much underground that we didn't know about, I presume.

I don't want to waste your time philosophizing. But I do want to say this one thing. We are in an awfully serious hour for Christianity, for our own souls. We are faced with necessity to be very faithful to the Law of Christ, and His truth. This means that we must do everything that we reasonably can to find our way peacefully through the mess we are in. This is becoming harder and harder every day and success seems less and less likely. Yet we remain responsible for doing the things that "are for our peace." ("Jerusalem, Jerusalem, if thou hadst known the things that are for thy peace . . . and now there shall not be left of thee a stone upon a stone.")

We have to be articulate and sane, and speak wisely on every occasion where we can speak, and to those who are willing to listen. That is why for one I speak to you. We have to try to some extent to preserve the sanity of this nation, and keep it from going berserk which will be its destruction, and ours, and perhaps also the destruction of Christendom.

I wanted to say these few things, as we enter the New Year. For it is going to be a crucial year, and in it we are going to have to walk sanely, and in faith, and with great sacrifice, and with an almost impossible hope.

10. TO WALTER STEIN

I have your letter of the 12th and am glad to hear from you. As I said in the letter to the people of the Merlin Press, I found the book edited by you very impressive. What struck me most was the fact that the level was high, the thinking was energetic and uncompromising, and I was stimulated by the absence of the familiar clichés, or by worn out mannerisms which have served us all in the evasion of real issues. For example (without applying these criticisms to any other book in particular) I was very struck by the superiority of your book over "Morals and Missiles" which nevertheless had some good things in it. But "Morals and Missiles" had that chatty informality which the Englishman of Chesterton's generation thought he had to adopt as a protection whenever he tried to speak his mind on anything serious. Thank God you have thrown that off, because it stifles a lot of very good thought. Many of us here feel that 1962 is going to be awfully critical. Humanly speaking, the mentality of this country as I now understand it, is utterly sinister, desperate, belligerent, illogical. We will either press the button or become fascists, in which case the button will be pressed all the more inevitably later on. The one hope is that a lot of people who have more sense are protesting and there is a real communication going on among them which is quite heartening. But one wonders just what can be done, when the country is in the grip of the business-military complex that lives on the weapons and is dominated by them. We have actually reached the state where our weapons are telling us what to do. We are guided, instructed and nurtured by our destructive machines.

II. TO A PROFESSOR OF HUMANITIES

It was kind of you to send me the remarkably good essay by Fr. Tavard. I have read it with considerable interest and will discuss it with the novices here. He is clear and positive and I think he says very much that can be helpful.

Certainly it is first of all important to realize that Christian culture poses a question, and constitutes a problem. Too often we start out with the assumption that all the answers are quite clear, and that we of course are the ones who know them. That everyone else is malicious or ignorant, and that all that is required is for everyone to listen to us and agree with us in everything from faith to table manners and taste in art. Then the world will be all right.

This attitude, as I feel, together with Fr. Tavard, is precisely the most fatal and the most absurd we can possibly take. It assumes that "Christendom" is as much a reality today as it was in the 13th century, or at any rate after the

Council of Trent, and that Catholic culture is the culture of those who are obviously and aggressively Catholic in the American sense of the word. We have failed to see that in that sense of the word, we have come to be living contradictions. The "Catholic" who is the aggressive specimen of a ghetto Catholic culture, limited, rigid, prejudiced, negative, is precisely a non-Catholic, at least in the cultural sense. Worse still, he may be anti-Catholic in the cultural sense and perhaps even, in some ways, religiously, without realizing it. Do you think this is too bold and too sweeping a statement? I know it would shock and hurt many, but still I think there is a lot of truth in it. And I think we sometimes obscurely realize it and this contributes no little to our guilt and aggressivity.

In any case I think Fr. Tavard's analysis is very acute, especially as regards the "cosmic" demands for catholicity. I agree too, of course, as anyone with eyes and ears must inevitably agree, that medieval "Christendom" has ceased to exist and that we are *bel et bien* in the post-Christian era culturally speaking. Unless we realize this fact, we cannot possibly make sense out of our situation and its claims upon us. Nor is it reasonable to expect the troubles of the world to be settled all of a sudden by miraculous mass conversion to what, for better or for worse, we actually have now in the way of Christian life, culture, etc., *on top of our faith.*

We just simply do not deserve this, nor would it be merciful of God to bring such a thing about. On the contrary, I am quite sure He wants to teach us much, our *Paidagogos,* and to teach us precisely by the exigencies of our terrible situation.

At one point I would amplify and clarify what Fr. Tavard has said: where he discusses Marx. He does not make clear the inner spiritual potentialities hidden under the surface of the Marxian dialectic and the genuine pretensions to humanism that Marx himself expressed. The subordination of man to the technological process is not something that Marx accepts with unqualified satisfaction. On the contrary it is, for him the danger and the challenge of a technology based on profit. He thought that the ultimate challenge was for man to free himself from his machines and gain control over them, thus breaking the bonds of alienation and making himself the master of his history. The early essays of Marx recently published by Erich Fromm (Praeger) have some interesting possibilities in the way of the kind of dialogue Fr. Tavard suggests. For in these early essays, in which Marx concentrates on the problem of alienation, there is a very clear demand for the kind of dimension that can only be supplied by wisdom. Marx himself was uncertain and ambiguous in his treatment of this, but in any case he finds himself compelled to toy with the idea of a human nature on which to base his humanism. Now of course to what extent his latent existentialism destroyed or fulfilled this is a question for experts. But in recent discussions among the "revisionists" in those iron curtain countries where the strict dogmatism of the Marxians is questioned, points like this are always agonizingly close to the surface.

Hence I would offer this as a further contribution to the question: if there is to be a collaboration between the Christian humanist and the technological humanist, based on the latter's eventual realization of the need for wisdom, this is going to require as of now a living and radical dialogue between Christian thinkers of the west and revisionist Marxists in the east. How this is to be brought about the Lord alone knows. It is however vitally important.

12. TO A RABBI

Many things: first I sent the books to Joe at the Kibbutz. I want to know a lot more about this Kibbutz.

I just got through reading *The Last of the Just*. I think it is a really great book. It has helped crystallize a whole lot of things I am thinking about.

Chief of these is of course no news to anyone: that the Jews are the great eschatalogical sign of the twentieth century. That everything comes to depend on people understanding this fact, not just reacting to it with a little appropriate feeling, but seeing the whole thing as a sign from God, telling us. Telling us what? Among other things, telling Christians that if they don't look out they are going to miss the boat or fall out of it, because the antinomy they have unconsciously and complacently supposed between the Jews and Christ is not even a very good figment of the imagination. The suffering Servant is One: Christ, Israel. There is one wedding and one wedding feast, not two or five or six. There is one bride. There is one mystery, and the mystery of Israel and of the Church is ultimately to be revealed as One. As one great scandal maybe to a lot of people on both sides who have better things to do than come to the wedding.

Of course it is in no sense a matter of shuttling back and forth institutionally. Each on our side must prepare for the great eschatalogical feast on the mountains of Israel.

Therefore I am not at all surprised that you like the *New Man,* the best parts of which are Old Testament parts.

When the Christians began to look at Christ as Prometheus . . . You see what I mean? Then they justified war, then they justified the crusades, then they justified pogroms, then they justified Auschwitz, then they justified the bomb, then they justified the Last Judgment: The Christ of Michelangelo is Prometheus, I mean the Christ in the Sistine Chapel. He is whipping sinners with his great Greek muscles. "All right," they say, "if we can't make it to the wedding feast (and they are the ones who refused) we can blow up the joint and say it is the Last Judgment." Well, that's how it is the Judgment, and that's the way men judge themselves, and that's the way the poor and the helpless and the maimed and the blind enter into the Kingdom: when the Prometheus types blow the door wide open for them.

Enough. More some other time. May we enter into the Kingdom and sit down with Abraham and Isaac and Jacob and the Holy One, Blessed be His Name, to whom Abraham gave hospitality in the Three Strangers.

13. TO SISTER M. MADELEVA

The chief reason why Julian of Norwich and the other English Mystics are not in the notes I sent, is that I did not have time to treat them adequately, and in proportion to my love for them. I also left out the Cistercians, practically. But Julian is without doubt one of the most wonderful of all Christian voices. She gets greater and greater in my eyes as I grow older and whereas in the old days I used to be crazy about St. John of the Cross, I would not exchange him now for Julian if you gave me the world and the Indies and all the Spanish mystics rolled up in one bundle. I think that Julian of Norwich is with Newman the greatest English theologian. She is really that. For she reasons from her experience of the substantial center of the great Christian mystery of Redemption. She gives her experience and her deductions, clearly, separating the two. And the experience is of course nothing merely subjective. It is the objective mystery of Christ as apprehended by her, with the mind and formation of a fourteenth century English woman. And that fourteenth century England is to me and always has been a world of light, for I have almost lived in it. So many villages and churches of the time are still there practically without change, or were thirty years ago.

14. TO CATHERINE DE HUECK
     DOHERTY

You ask me if I am weary? Sure. Perhaps not as weary as you are, but weary in the same way, weary of the same things. The weariness is compounded by the fact that one is tempted to feel he has no right to be weary of the actions and pronouncements of a lot of very good, sincere people who are themselves weary of something or other that is odious to them. We are like a bunch of drunken men at the last end of a long stupid party falling over the furniture in the twilight of dawn. I hope it is dawn.

It is at such a time as this that one has to have faith in the Church, and the fact that we suffer from the things that make us suffer, the fact that we cannot find any way out of the suffering, is perhaps a sign of hope. I do not pretend to understand the situation or to analyze anything. Your answer is correct. What is wanted is love. But love has been buried under words, noise, plans, projects, systems, and apostolic gimmicks. And when we open our mouths to do something about it we add more words, noise, plans, etc. We are afflicted with the disease of constant talking with almost nothing to say. From that point of view I suppose it is just as well that I am saying nothing more about the war business. Saying things does not help. Yet what is there to do? You're right again, that what one must do is meet the needs that God brings before us, when and as He does so. We will not see anything clear, but we must do His will. We have to be heroic in our obedience to God.

And that may mean cutting through a whole forest of empty talk, clichés and nonsense just to begin to find some glimmer of His will. To obey always and not know for sure if we are really obeying. That is not fun at all, and people like to get around the responsibility by entering into a routine of trivialities in which everything seems clear, noble and defined: but when you look at it honestly it falls apart, for it is riddled with absurdity from top to bottom.

15. TO DR. JOHN C. H. WU

I had better get this letter written before any more time flows under the bridge (what bridge? what time? this is our illusion). But in any case time has something to do with the fact that I am going to say Mass for your intentions on June 15th, a week from tomorrow, which will be Friday in Whitsun week, and I shall be praying that you obtain not only that gift of the Holy Ghost which is assigned by St. Andrew's missal for that day (whatever ideas the St. Andrew's missal may have on the subject, and I don't especially care) but for you to receive all the gifts in all abundance and all the fruits and beatitudes and the Holy Spirit Himself in incomprehensible fulness. This Mass is being said for you at the request of Mrs.

O'Brian and I promised her.a long time ago I would let you know. We don't have, or seem not to have, those little Mass cards around here, so I am sending you a letter. In fact it finally occurs to me that in this matter of saying Masses and getting notices out to people about it I am at the topmost peak of inefficiency and I do not know how I survive in the American Church with such slapdash methods: I just say Mass for people when I get a chance. Primitive, almost heretical.

But it will be a joy to stand in the presence of the Heavenly Father, in Christ, and speak of you and all whom you love and of China.

Paul Sih has obtained for me a wonderful reprint of the Legge translation of the Chinese Classics, and has also sent the Wang Yang Ming. I am awed and delighted with the great volumes of the Classics. I do not intend to read them lightly however, and they are waiting until other things can be cleared away. But I must admit I have done absolutely no work at all on Chinese, because I find that I simply waste too much time fumbling around in the dictionary and so little is done that it does not make sense to continue until some time in the future when I can get some instruction. So it will all have to wait a bit. I am working on the Latin Fathers, with whom I can make enough headway to know what is happening. Perhaps I shall do a translation of an excerpt from Cassiodorus. I think you would like him. He is very much the Confucian scholar, Latin style. A great librarian and student and copyist of books but also a polished writer and an engaging thinker, besides a man of prayer. His monastery of Vivarium was most attractive: it was a monastery of scholars.

And now to turn suddenly from scholarship to less pleasant subjects. I hesitate to send you the enclosed angry and bitter poem. It is savage, and its savagery hits everything in sight, so that it is not kind to anyone, even to the poor sad desperate Chinese girl whose picture broke my heart and suggested the poem. I wish I could have said something full of mercy and love that would have been worthy of the situation, but I have only used her plight to attack the hypocrisy of those who find no room for the Chinese refugees, and who always have a very good reason for saying "No" to human suffering. And the sad plight of a whole society which nods approval, while pronouncing a few polite formulas of regret. I suppose I should not get angry, and that it represents a weakness in myself to get excited still about the sickening inhumanities that are everywhere in the world. They are too awful for human protest to be meaningful,—or so people seem to think. I protest anyway, I am still primitive enough, I have not caught up with this century.

16. TO A NEW CONVERT

What can I tell you about the Church? You have been very patient with her human deficiencies, and that patience is also her gift. Your letter reflects the extraordinary serenity with which the new convert accepts *everything*. And one has to. In a sense it is true that one only comes in with blinders on, blinders one has put on and kept on. One has to refuse to be disturbed by so many things. And you are right in the refusal. These are temporal and absurd matters which, in the eschatalogical perspectives, which are the true ones, must vanish forever along with many other things that are more precious and far from absurd in themselves.

The Church is not of this world, and she complacently reminds us of this when we try to budge her in any direction. But on the other hand we in the world are of the Church and we also have our duty to speak up and say the Church is not of this world when her refusal turns out, in effect, to be a refusal to budge from a solidly and immovably worldly position. The urgency with which I have shouted what I wanted to say is due to the fact that I knew I would not go on shouting for very long and indeed the shouting is already over. You may perhaps see an issue of Blackfriars one of these days with the last echo of my outcry.

But to get back to you and Emy, I am so happy for you. Be true to the Spirit of God and to Christ. Read your prophets sometimes, and go through the Gospels and St. Paul and see what is said there: that is your life. You are called to a totally new, risen, transformed life in the Spirit of Christ. A life of simplicity and truth and joy that is not of this world. May you be blessed always in it, you and the children. I send you all my love and blessings.

17. TO A QUAKER

Thank you for writing to me. I feel very close indeed to the Friends and I always have, so you must not feel embarrassed about the difference in our religious affiliations. Besides you have read many books that are very much in line with the kind of contemplative life we have here. Dom Chapman is especially good. Caussade is, of course, a master.

Naturally the idea of a "Church" supposes that we all have an ingrained need for one another and that we all aspire by a kind of basic instinct of grace to a community in which the Spirit of

Christ will speak to us and guide us. However there are groups and groups, and community life is now more and now less transparent a medium for the action of the Holy Spirit. You must not be surprised or sad if in your prayer group your own aspirations are not understood. It is neither possible nor easy to find understanding when you travel a rather lonely way.

We can always say that the way of the contemplative should not be unusual or lonely, and that for him to think of it as unusual is doubtless risky. But the facts are there and so is the experience.

It remains for you to trust God, not to make you infallible but to protect you from serious error and to make good the smaller mistakes. And thus with confidence in His guidance, even though you may not always interpret it correctly, you can advance peacefully. I am sure He will guide you safely in everything if you take care to keep your heart quiet and pure, as best you can, and listen to His voice in simplicity, trying to avoid the more obvious illusions, and keeping as close as possible to the solid bedrock of faith. With that, He will do all the rest. And He will put books into your hands that will tell you what your friends cannot.

I am a bad correspondent, but if you ever need me, please write.

18. TO FRIENDS OF VICTORIA OCAMPO (FOR A COMMEMORATIVE VOLUME)

I wonder if there is anyone in the world of western culture today who does not know Victoria Ocampo, and who has not come within the sphere of her radiance. She is one of those wonderful people who includes in herself all the grace and wisdom of a universal culture at a given time. I advisedly refrain from using the word cosmopolitan, which in an age of tourism has been reduced to meaninglessness and vulgarity. In a sense she is a model for all of us in the breadth of her interests, her sympathies, and her capacity for sensitive understanding. She is in our age of miraculous communications, miraculously a person who has something to communicate. The rest of us, perhaps, use our fantastic instruments merely to echo one anothers' noise. And communication must always fulfill one essential condition if it is to exist at all: it must be human, it must have resonances that are deeper than formal statements, declarations and manifestoes. And yet at the same time one of the great things about Doña Victoria is that if an intelligent manifesto is still possible, somewhere, somehow, one is likely to see her name on it. I do not make this as a statement of accurate fact, as I am in no position to follow all the manifestoes and declarations that are made: but simply as a kind of poetic truth about Doña Victoria. She is a symbol of the bright and articulate judgement of a cultured person. To me she symbolizes America in the broad sense, the only sense, in which I am proud to be numbered among Americans. I am honored and delighted to join all those who, in proclaiming their admiration and love for her, are thereby taking what may perhaps be one of the final opportunities left to men to declare themselves civilized.

19. TO A CONTEMPLATIVE NUN

This is not an adequate letter, but I do want to get some kind of reply into the mail for you, as the project of the "Retiro" sounds most interesting. It is something that deserves every possible encouragement and I want to do my bit. I will try to remember to fill an envelope with materials that might be of use to you and get it off in the next couple of days. You can guess however that I have not much time for handling mail, and secretarial help is strictly limited.

Transformation in Christ is a difficult book, and I let the novices read it, without however pushing them. On the other hand Von Hildebrand's *Defense of Purity* is, it seems to me, a superbly spiritual treatment of chastity. There is a lot about marriage in it, but I feel the novices ought to appreciate the married state which they are renouncing. What good to renounce it if they do not know its dignity? For a "retiro" however the needs might be different.

Bouyer on the *Meaning of the Monastic Life* we regard as standard. In an older context, there is Dom Marmion, always safe and solid. Bouyer's new *Introduction to Spirituality* is considered radical by some, but I should think you might be able to use it. A perfect biography of St. Therese which is very useful for all religious is the *Hidden Face* by Goerres. We always like Guardini here. To my mind he is one of the most important and articulate Catholic authors of the moment. He has good things on prayer, faith, and so on. *Prayer in Practice* comes to mind as excellent. Fr. Danielou is liked by the novices and I like him too.

These are just a few books that spring to mind as I write. I will try to dig up one of our novitiate reading lists and put it in the envelope I hope to send.

I remember St. Elizabeth's well, and you have a lovely place for a cloistered contemplative life— except perhaps for the trains, but who cares about a few trains once in a while? Are you right in the old convent, or are you somewhere apart?

Remember that in the enclosed and solitary life, your solitude itself will do an immense amount for you. The sisters need not strain and struggle and worry too much about "degrees" of prayer. The great thing is to be emptied out, to taste and see that the Lord is sweet, and to learn the way of abandonment and peace. Littleness is the chief characteristic of the solitary, or else he is not a genuine solitary. Silence is a rare luxury in the modern world, and not everyone can stand it: but it has inestimable value, that cannot be purchased with any amount of money or power or intelligence. The gift to be silent and simple with the Lord is a treasure beyond counting and it almost takes care of everything else, at least in some souls.

20. TO A CHINESE PRIEST IN CALIFORNIA

Your friendly letter has waited about a month for an answer, and I have been taking it very seriously. I do want to help you if I can, in any work involving Asian students.

Your idea of the Christian Unity Corps sounds really fine, and I especially like the last part, about

Catholic American families giving hospitality to Asian students. I believe that the Asian, South American and African students are in a way the most important people in the world today. They have magnificent potentialities. They also face tremendous dangers.

Let me say this: I do not know if I have anything to offer to Asians but I am convinced that I have an immense amount to learn from Asia. One of the things I would like to share with Asians is not only Christ but Asia itself. I am convinced that a rather superficial Christianity in European dress is not enough for Asia. We have lacked depth. We have lacked the breadth of view to grasp all the wonderful breadth and richness in the Asian traditions, which were given to China, India, Japan, Korea, Burma, etc. as natural preparations for the coming of Christ. I feel that often those who finally brought Christ may have fallen short of the preparation that the Holy Spirit had provided and hence Our Lord was not seen in all His divine splendor.

Yet at the same time I fully realize the complexity of the problem today. The Asians have renounced Asia. They want to be western, sometimes they are frantic about being western. They want to go places. They feel that there have been centuries of inertia and stagnation, and there is a reaction against the humiliations and misunderstandings of colonialism, calling for a defeat of the west at its own technological game. All this is dangerous but inevitable. Christianity of course has a crucial part to play in saving all that is valuable in the east as well as in the west.

21.   TO FRANK SHEED

I have been reading Gordon Zahn's book, *German Catholics and Hitler's Wars,* which you published. It is a most important and very competent job of work. It deserves far more than the obvious platitudes which spring to mind about any good new book. To say that it raises a vitally important issue is so far short of doing it justice that it is ridiculous.

It raises an issue that most of us are frankly incapable of understanding or even thinking about intelligently. It goes terribly deep, and much too deep for the average Catholic, the average priest, the average bishop. Zahn is objective with scientific innocence. There is no guile in his approach. He just says what he says, and overstates nothing. Where the impact comes is in the delayed action after one has read a chapter or so. Then all of a sudden one comes to with a jolt and says to himself: "This really means that something very dreadful is happening and has been happening, and that the bottom is dropping out of what we

have been accustomed to regard as a fully satisfactory and complete picture of Christianity, or
Christian civilization. Perhaps it has already
dropped. . . ." That is a mixed metaphor no
doubt. The bottom drops out of a bucket, not of
a picture. But perhaps one tends to feel that the
picture iself has just dropped out of a frame.

Then the Hans Küng book, *The Council,
Reform and Reunion*. This too is splendid. One's
reaction is more hopeful and more positive. But
the sense of urgency remains the same. This Council has got to fulfill great hopes or be a disaster.
There is absolutely no use in reaffirming the
disciplinary and juridical positions that have been
affirmed one way or another for a thousand years.
This is not reform, not renewal. That is what
comes out of these two books, with great force.
We are no longer living in the world of Gregory
VII or Innocent III or Pius V, or even Pius X.
To be a perfect Christian, even a saint according
to their pattern, is no longer enough. To attempt
it may involve us in fatal illusions!

22. TO A BENEDICTINE
STUDYING IN GERMANY

I certainly envy you going to study under
Küng at Tubingen. I am finishing his *The Council, Reform and Reunion* and it is one of the

most exciting books I have read in years. There is really a breath of new life about this book and about his outlook. It is awake and frank, not wild, but objectively Catholic in the finest sense—not the sense of the poor good people who have been paralyzed for ages by rigidities and conventions. A book like this makes one realize many many things. It enables one to judge and to accept many things that were felt heretofore in the conscience only as obscure and ambiguous gnawings.

It is then quite true that we are right to feel so uncomfortable and so terribly beaten down by the old negative, falsely conservative and authoritarian spirit that purely and simply clings to the status quo for its own sake.

It is quite true that so many things that we have feared to call dead, are really dead after all. "Why do you seek the dead among the living?" There is after all something to the spiritual and Churchly sense which remains uneasy and crippled under the burden of what have to be frankly admitted as "dead works." Also evasions and even dishonesties, not perhaps fully conscious ones.

Realizing this does not make one proud and rebellious. It is a chastening and humbling experience. One sees that so many people, in good faith, and with subjectively good reasons, are clinging to ways of life and ways of seeing life which lead to spiritual blindness and which almost choke the life out of the faithful. Hence the priestly mentality that comes out of so many seminaries. The beaten-down bright subservience and cultivated stupidity of the Catholic layman. The official, managerial insolence and self-complacency of some of those in authority. The diplomacies, the subterfuges, the wiles, the manipulations of the law to keep people "quiet and happy."

When one sees all this frankly, he realizes that he himself is likewise involved, likewise at fault. One does not have temptations to rise up and shatter it all with violent criticism, on the contrary. One feels the need to meditate and do penance interiorly, to keep silent until such time as one or two quiet words may be indicated by grace. One wants to obey with a new seriousness and responsibility, seeing at the same time with clearer eyes what one is about, and seeing the limitations and deficiencies in which one is oneself involved.

Obviously Christian humility is not purely the humility of the subject who is always wrong before the official who is always right, but something far deeper, far nobler and more human: the humility of the member of Christ who realizes that he and all the other members are so unworthy of their Head in so many ways, and yet that they can help one another by honesty and humility to be more worthy of the Spirit Who is given to them all.

Thanks for the material on Una Sancta and Fr. Metzger's prison letters, I have not plunged into these yet, it will take time. I want to write a bit more about him and make him known: a great man, one of the *seven* who, out of so many thousands in the German peace movement, continued to stick to his principles after Hitler, long enough and uncompromisingly enough to pay for them with his life. That too is terribly significant, a strangely meaningful chapter in the history of the Church.

23. TO MARK VAN DOREN

Here, a poem. That is all. I have no other pretext for writing, but am glad to have this one. It is a poem about a drawing of a house by a five year old child. What a drawing, what a house, what suns and birds! It is true that we do not know where we are.

That there are circles within circles, and that if we choose we can let loose in the circle of paradise the very wrath of God: this is said by Boehme in his confessions. We are trying to bear him out. Children can, if they still will, give us the lie and show us our folly. But we are now more and more persistent in refusing to see any such thing. All we will see is the image, the imago, the absurd spectre, the mask over our own emptiness. And we will beat on the box to make the voice come out. And it will speak numbers to us, oracular numbers, delphic billions this way and that way.

I have read a little of Thoreau and know enough to lament that such good sense died so long ago. But it could still be ours if only we wanted it. We do not, we want the image, the consuming image, the dead one into which we pour soft drinks. The smiles of the image. All the girls are laughing because the image has a soft drink. He will, with the power of the drink, explode a moon.

So let the moons explode and the books be silent. Let the captains whirl in the sky, let the monkeys in the heavens move levers with hands and feet, and with their big toe explode cities, for a soft drink.

I know this is the wrong kind of image. I have rebelled against an image. This is not safe, is it? Well, alas, so I must reconcile myself to the unsafe, because the safe I can no longer stomach.

Let them beat on the box while the noise comes out in a stream of lighted numbers. I have resigned from numbers.

24.   TO SPANISH SEMINARIANS

Time does not permit me to answer your question at length, and perhaps I am not well qualified to do so, as I live a cloistered life. Yet since it is true that every Christian, including the contemplatives, must also be in some sense apostles, the question of the Christian missions is of course very close to my heart.

The missionary, like every Apostle, has the duty to bring to people everywhere not only a doctrine, but the Person of the Holy Spirit, the Life-giving Paraclete Who makes Christ live in the minds and hearts of men. It is thus that the Missionary completely fulfills his task of "preaching Christ crucified." Naturally this mission remains always a scandal: but perhaps it has in the course of centuries become a scandal in ways we do not clearly realize. The message of Christ may be a scandal not only to the ones who are supposed to receive it, but it may also be one to those who preach it. That is to say that the Missionary himself may be the first to "stumble" over the awful exigency of the demand of the Savior to "leave all." He must leave his habits of thought and the outlook of his native land, and must seek to bring the message of Christ to other peoples in terms familiar *to them*. There is always a danger that instead of preaching the Gospel we preach and even attempt to impose the standards of our own society and culture, which may or may not be very Christian.

In any case the Missionary must surrender himself totally to Christ and the Church, and abandon himself to the will of God. For this he must have a deep interior life and a great love for the Cross and for souls.

There are many other aspects of this question that could be treated, but I am sure that the Ecumenical Council will, guided by the Holy Spirit, make known to us far deeper truths than I could suggest. We must expect these new clarifications eagerly, in all the fields where they will apply: liturgy, seminary training, the task of the religious and secular institutes, etc.

May God Bless you in your studies and investigations of these questions so important to His Church. Pray for all whom He will call to this great work. I will remember you at the Holy Sacrifice. Pray for me.

25. TO THE HON. SHINZO HAMAI, MAYOR OF HIROSHIMA

In a solemn and grave hour for humanity, I address this letter to you and to your people. I thank you for the sincerity and courage with which you are, at this time, giving witness for peace and sanity. I wish to join my own thoughts, efforts and prayers to yours. There is no hope for mankind unless truth prevails in us. We must purify our hearts and open them to the light of truth and mercy. You are giving us the example. May we follow.

I speak to you as a most humble and unworthy brother, a monk of a contemplative Order of the Catholic Church. As such, I have learned to have a very great love for Japan and for its spiritual traditions. There are in Japan several convents and one monastery of my religious Order. The Japanese Trappistine nuns are the glory of our Order. The finest and most fervent of our convents are those in Japan. May their whole-hearted prayers for peace and for the spiritual and temporal prosperity of your nation be heard.

Men should use political instruments in behalf of truth, sanity, and international order. Unfortunately the blindness and madness of a society that is shaken to its very roots by the storm of passion and greed for power make the fully effective use of political negotiation impossible. Men want to negotiate for peace, and strive to do so, but their fear is greater than their good will. They do not dare to take serious and bold initiatives for peace. Fear of losing face, fear of the propaganda consequences of apparent "weakness," make it impossible for them to do what is really courageous: to take firm steps towards world peace. When they take one step forward they immediately tell the whole world about it and then take four steps backwards. We are all walking backwards towards a precipice. We know the precipice is there, but we assert that we are all the while going forward. This is because the world in its madness is guided by military men, who are the blindest of the blind.

It is my conviction that the people of Hiroshima stand today as a symbol of the hopes of humanity. It is good that such a symbol should exist. The event of August 6th 1945 gives you the most solemn right to be heard and respected by the whole world. But the world only pretends to respect your witness. In reality it cannot face the truth which you represent. But I wish to say on my own behalf and on behalf of my fellow monks and those who are like-minded, that I never cease to face the truth which is symbolized in the names Hiroshima, Nagasaki. Each day I pray humbly and with love for the victims of the atomic bombardments which took place there. All the holy spirits of those who lost their lives then, I regard as my dear and real friends. I express my fraternal and humble love for all the citizens of Hiroshima and Nagasaki.

26. TO A SCHOLAR

Certainly I think I owe a great deal to Léon Bloy's writings. I do not remember how I first discovered him: doubtless through some mention made by one of the Maritains. I remember at Columbia in the late '30s, I used to draw on the rather large collection of Bloy in the library, and the only other person who was using the books at the time was Raissa Maritain, whose name appeared next to mine on the cards.

Perhaps Bloy's intransigence appealed to a youthful element of extremism in my own personality: but at any rate it seemed to me that his demand for a completely revolutionary and radical form of Christianity was the only way to redeem the comfortable and evasive Christianity of modern times from its total and sometimes blasphemous lack of seriousness. I do not think that Bloy's language is always perfectly balanced or measured. He is extreme, and sometimes carried away by rage that may or may not always be prophetic. That is not the point. To demand that Bloy speak like a pontiff, in serene and placid periods, is to demand that he be someone else than Bloy. And as a writer he is sometimes magnificent, especially in his indignation.

Perhaps what I owe him more than anything

else is contact with La Salette. I was most deeply moved by *"Celle qui Pleure."* Perhaps it has meant more to me than any other book of his. It obviously had a great deal to do with a poem on La Salette that I wrote later and which appeared in my book, *Figures for an Apocalypse*. I think that whole book, in its qualities and in its weaknesses, is marked by the influence of Bloy. And that brings out the fact that it is perhaps too easy and too automatic for me to be indignant, and that Bloy is something I have had to "outgrow" in the sense of not according him a servile veneration (which he would not have wanted anyway). Perspective however has only increased my respect for him and my compassion for his sufferings in his great and fruitful vocation. It was inevitable that he be accused of everything heinous: he was too rabidly outspoken for any other fate. But he is, to my mind, an example of furious integrity and a figure of great religious importance for our time. I do not think he ever claimed the charism of infallibility and hence one can reserve the right to disagree with some of his opinions, in detail. But too great an anxiety to dot all the "i"'s and cross all the "t"'s may make one overlook the fact that his vision of our age has been not only prophetic but in its horror has even fallen *short of the truth*. Far, far short.

I would add that there are some remarks about

"The Woman who was Poor" and perhaps other allusions to Bloy in my *Secular Journal,* which was much influenced in some respects, by Bloy's Journals which I was reading at that time. I forgot if I refer to this in the preface. I do not have a copy here to check.

Yes, Dame Kristine did write and I was glad to hear from her. I am glad that Canon Christiani showed some willingness to modify and retract his sweeping judgments of Bloy borrowed from questionable authors. [Canon L. Christiani had repeated some irresponsible rumors that Bloy was a "satanist."]

27. TO A MOSLEM

I received your two books safely—the *Saints and Shrines* and the biographies. I am especially interested in the latter, which are in many cases remarkable. I thank you very much for these two books. The "Shrines" will answer many future questions about holy places and pilgrimages in Islam, a most absorbing topic.

The departure of Louis Massignon is a great and regrettable loss. He was a man of great comprehension and I was happy to have been numbered among his friends, for this meant entering into an almost prophetic world, in which he habitually moved. It seems to me that mutual comprehension between Christians and Moslems is something of very vital importance today, and unfortunately it is rare and uncertain, or else subjected to the vagaries of politics. I am touched by the deep respect and understanding which so many Moslems had for him. Indeed they understood him and appreciated his work perhaps better than many Christians.

I am not surprised at your great interest in St. John of the Cross. The question of detachment depends it seems to me first of all on self knowledge. Or rather the two are mutually interdependent. One must know what are the real attachments in his soul before he can effectively work against them, and one must have a detached will in order to see the truth of one's attachments. In practice, the events of life bring us face to face, in painful situations, with the places in which we are attached to our inner egoism. I think it is necessary for us to see that God Himself works to purify us of our inner "self" that tends to resist Him and to assert itself against Him. Our faith must teach us to see His will and to bend to His will precisely in those points where He attacks the self, even through the actions of other people. Here the unjust and unkind actions of others, even though objectionable in themselves can strip us of interior attachment.

Also St. John of the Cross makes much out of the purifying effect of aridity and helplessness in prayer: which is very beneficial to us if it leads to an increase of faith. I think here the important point is now to discuss the relation between the concept of faith for a Christian and a corresponding concept for a Moslem. This is probably where a deep divergence may be found, though perhaps not as deep as I anticipate.

I will be interested to hear from you further on this point, and will also keep it in mind myself.

No, the portrait of the saint in *Counsels of Light and Love* is purely fanciful and is indeed not a good portrait of anything. I will try to find a picture of St. John that is more genuine, and will send it. Perhaps I can enclose it in this letter.

Now, I must close: yes, I have remembered you most particularly in prayer in this season of prayer and hope you also will remember me in the holy season of Ramanan and on the Night of Destiny. I shall keep you in my prayers also as time proceeds.

28.   TO JAMES BALDWIN

You cannot expect to write as you do without getting letters like this. One has to write, and I am sure you have received lots of letters already that say better than I can what this will try to say.

First of all, you are right all down the line. You exaggerate nowhere. You know exactly what you are talking about, and as a matter of fact it is really news to nobody (that is precisely one of your points). I have said the same myself, much more mildly and briefly, and far less well, in print so it is small wonder that I agree with you.

But the point is that this is one of the great realities of our time. For Americans it is perhaps the crucial truth, and all the other critical questions that face us are involved in this one.

It is certainly matter for joy that you have at least said so much, and in the place where you have said it. It will be read and understood. But as I went through column after column I was struck, as I am sure you were, by the ads all along each side of your text. What a commentary! They prove you more right than you could have imagined. They go far beyond anything you have said. What force they lend to all your statements. No one could have dreamed up more damning evidence to illustrate what you say.

Sometimes I am convinced that there cannot be a way out of this. Humanly there is no hope, at least on the white side (that is where I unfortunately am). I don't see any courage or any capacity to grasp even the smallest bit of the enormous truth about ourselves. Note, I speak as a Catholic priest. We still see the whole thing as a sort of abstract exercise in ethics, when we see it at all. We don't see we are killing our own hope and the hope of the world.

You are very careful to make explicit the non-Christian attitude you take, and I respect this because I understand that this is necessary for you and I do not say this as an act of tolerant indulgence. It is in some sense necessary for me, too, because I am only worth so much as a priest, as I am able to see what the non-Christian sees. I am in most things right with you and the only point on which I disagree is that I think your view is fundamentally religious, genuinely religious, and therefore has to be against conventional religiosity. If you do not agree it does not matter very much.

The other day I was talking to an African priest from Ghana. The impression I always get in talking to Africans is that they have about ten times as much reality as we have. This of course is not an accurate way of speaking: I think what it really expresses, this "sense," is the awareness of complementarity, the awareness of a reality in him which completes some lack in myself, and not of course an intuition of an absolute ontological value of a special essence. And I think as you yourself have suggested, that this is the whole story: there is not one of us, individually, racially, socially, who is fully complete in the sense of having in himself *all* the excellence of all humanity. And that this excellence, this totality, is built up out of the contributions of the particular parts of it that we all can share wih one another. I am therefore not completely human until I have found myself in my African and Asian and Indonesian brother because he has the part of humanity which I lack.

The trouble is that we are supposed to be, and in a way we are, complete in ourselves. And we cherish the illusion that this completeness is not just a potential, but that is finally realized from the very start, and that the notion of having to find something of ourselves only after a long search and after the gift of ourselves to others, does not apply to us. This illusion, which makes the white man imagine he does not need the Negro, enables him to think he can treat the Negro as an "object" and do what he likes with him. Indeed, in order to prove that his illusion is true, he goes ahead and treats the Negro in the way we know. He has to.

At the heart of the matter then is man's contempt for truth, and the substitution of his "self" for reality. His image is his truth. He believes in his specter and sacrifices human beings to his specter. This is what we are doing, and this is not Christianity or any other genuine religion: it is barbarity.

We cannot afford to have contempt for any truth, but least of all for a truth as urgent in our lives as this one. Hence, I want to give you all the moral support I can, which isn't much. I know you are more than fatigued with well-meaning white people clapping you on the shoulder and saying with utmost earnestness "We are right with you" when of course we are right with ourselves and not in any of the predicaments you are in at all. What I will say is that I am glad I am not a Negro because I probably would never be able to take it: but that I recognize in conscience that I have a duty to try to make my fellow whites stop doing the things they do and see the problem in a different light. This does not presuppose an immediate program or a surge of optimism, because I am still convinced that there is almost nothing to be done that will have any deep effect or make any real difference.

I am not in a position to be completely well informed on this issue, anyway. If you think of anything I ought to know about, I would be grateful if you put it in an envelope and send it down. I hope your article will have done some good. The mere fact that truth has been told is already a very great good in itself.

29. TO JEAN AND HILDEGARD
GOSS-MAYR

The great march in Washington was in many ways triumphant, and it was certainly a magnificent expression of restraint, dignity, good order. The nobility of the thousands of Negro participants was evident in the highest degree, and when they "thanked the white people" who were there, one of my friends broke down in tears. Really, for the whites who participated, it was a very great grace, and something they needed. Indeed they needed this chance to give some sign of repentance, much more than the Negro needed to have them there. In fact, politically, the presence of these white people was perhaps not entirely an advantage to the Negro because it tended to confuse the real situation just a little. Everything that tends to preserve the atmosphere of illusion, the false optimism which supposes that the Negro has a place all ready for him in white America; once more strengthens the inertia of those attached to a status quo in which, in fact, the Negro has no place whatever. He is an outcast. You would be horrified to know to what extent even in the Negro ghettoes the Negro is oppressed and exploited by white men, even to the extent that it is very difficult for a Negro to own a store or run a business of any consequence in the Negro ghetto, where the white shopkeepers bleed him with usury. This situation is very grave indeed and it is slowly creeping towards revolution of the violent kind, I very much fear. Yet the greatness of people like Martin Luther King is something to hope in and trust in. God can certainly use such men to work miracles, and perhaps He will. Indeed He already has.

30.   TO A WHITE PRIEST

You are defending a point of view that is taken for granted by practically everyone—except by the Negro who has a diametrically opposite view. The point of view you expressed is expressed in all the papers, on all the radios, in all the magazines, in all conversations, and it is that of the vast majority of Catholics. Hence there is no desperate need for it to be given a "hearing." It has one. It is the other view that does not have a hearing, and is having a terrible time getting one.

What everyone takes for granted is that the race question, though unpleasant and tense, though filled with regrettable and even unjust incidents, is something that has a solution waiting for it in the near future. That solution presupposes that the Negro has a place open and waiting in our society, and that given a little time, a little more legislation, a little more editorializing, and some increased good will, it will simply and naturally open itself up and then the Negro will be fitted in to the society we have and know. Everything will then go on as usual. Consequently, in this context, all that is needed is a little patience, together with charity and mutual understanding all round.

There can be no question that patience, charity and understanding are most urgently needed and required. No one is questioning the need of these values. The real question is: how and where are they *most* needed?

At the present time the word "patience" has been used and abused to cover every kind of inaction, foot dragging, double crossing, and political shilly-shallying so that when a person says "patience" to the Negro now, the Negro simply dismisses his statement as meaningless. This is not to say that patience is not needed, but only that the current talk about patience is so irrelevant that it is time to drop it and approach the topic from a different angle, and one that gets a little nearer the heart of the matter.

Here are some of the points that I think are ignored, while to ignore them is really a disaster for Catholics, for the Church, for the Negro and for the country.

1) The race question cannot be settled without a profound change of heart, a real shake-up and deep reaching *metanoia* on the part of White America. It is not just question of a little more good will and generosity: it is question of waking up to crying injustices and deep-seated problems which are ingrained in the present setup and which, instead of getting better, are going to get worse. The only way to prevent this from generating the worst kind of race hatreds and violence on both sides is to admit the existence of the problems in all their seriousness, and the consequent resolution to *share* the benefits of our society with the Negro as far as we can: that is to say, really give him equal opportunities in everything. If this happens, it is going to mean a real upheaval in the job situation and that is why people cannot begin to face it.

2) As to our Catholic Bishops and clergy, we must face the fact that whether they realize it or not, some of us are giving the *most grave kind of scandal,* scandal that will alienate people by the thousands from Christ and His Church, and is already doing so. This scandal is given, not consciously or willingly perhaps, but because the clergy are afraid of antagonizing rich and powerful groups or influential sectors of society (especially in the South), even though these people have been responsible for injustices and even crimes that cry

out to heaven for vengeance. To support such people and go along with them is in point of fact to collaborate in their injustices.

It is for this reason that I said that a priest or layman who is aware of the situation is placed in great moral peril for his soul. He has a very difficult dilemma to face. He has to take into account the rights of his superior and of obedience, but he must also recognize the danger of offending against the law of God Himself by becoming a collaborator in injustice and scandal. Thus it can hardly be said that such a one is obliged to practice the kind of monastic obedience that is counseled to those seeking perfection in an ideally constituted ascetic milieu.

In such a case I think that to practice passive patience and "blind obedience" would not be genuinely prudent. What is to be recommended is not resignation and passivity, handing over responsibility to the Superior and forgetting about the whole issue, but on the contrary a clear-eyed, watchful prudence, with constant statements of the facts as one sees them, in order in every possible way to clarify the issue and help the Superior to see it for what it really is. This is extremely difficult, and it is hard to see where one can begin when there is such fantastic ignorance about the whole issue in the first place.

3) Patience: certainly patience is required in

the case where imprudent and violent action will alienate and *antagonize potential supporters*. Here you have a real problem. There *are* men of good will around, and they do want to understand and to help. It is going to be hard for them to see the issue, and it will take time. But the fact remains that events are moving inexorably forward and they will not leave us time. We have to do everything we possibly can to help men of good will to understand the grave seriousness of the hour and the need for a total revaluation of the problem by the white man and particularly by the Catholic.

But we have to face the fact that soon the problem is likely to reach the point where it will so frighten most people, who have no way of understanding how it got that way, that they will be driven back in confusion into a blind and violent reaction, and this may lead to the worst kind of injustices, even to an American brand of Nazism. It has to be seen, however, that the use of the word patience at the present time to justify *inaction* is doing more than anything else to bring this about.

31. TO A GREEK WRITER

I am deeply moved by the seriousness and pathos of your poem. It tells something of the difficulty and the ambiguity of religion in our day.

There used to be a time when everybody thought that religion brought peace of heart, and indeed in this country some ministers were even preaching that faith would cure anxiety. But I think anyone who takes seriously the meaning of Christ in our world realizes that now the time has come when religion brings interior conflict. If we are resigned to spiritual inertia, Christ cannot live in us. He lives in us only in so far as we embrace the obligation to resist the inertia of secular society, and resist the appeals of a superficial and exterior world. At the same time it is no longer possible to fall back into a comfortable and spiritual realm that is consoling and delightful. What has gone is not God but Plato: there are no ideal worlds left, and man must realize that he is not just a "soul." This is the tragic thing for our religion, because we live in an age where the much more difficult task is not that of having a pure soul but also that of spiritualizing matter.

Here is where I think there are great possibilities in the Greek Orthodox tradition: the theology of St. Gregory Palamas, for example, with the belief in the "divine energies" and their transfiguring effect in the world of matter. This has not yet been explored, and I think a great work will be done when the hidden possibilities of this theology are made known to the world.

I was very happy to learn that Sefaris had won

the Nobel Prize. From what I know of him he is a very great poet, and I hope he will soon be translated into English.

32.   TO JACQUES MARITAIN

I have been planning to write and thank you for the new edition of Raissa's *Journal* which arrived, and is splendid. I will go through it again at leisure and in doing so will be near both you and her, and God too I am sure, for we can only be truly near one another in Him.

Then today your deeply moving letter arrived. I have never experienced such a thing as the spiritual crisis into which the violent death of President Kennedy has thrown the entire nation. It is not only profound but in many ways uncanny, for it is almost an apocalyptic event, a revelation of most powerful forces of evil and of very living forces of good that try to counteract them in this nation. The incredulity of the nation was the first thing that manifested itself: I do not mean lack of faith, I mean the incapacity to realize that the President was really dead and that this had been the result of a completely evil act which was itself the product of the evil in the heart of many Americans. In a word what has shattered the nation has been the realization of the awful presence of a very well-developed evil, a kind of spiritual cancer, at work in its very heart. No longer possible to situate all evil on the other side of the Iron Curtain!

At the same time, there has been frank and cynical rejoicing in the South, not of course everywhere, but among the racists, over the death of Kennedy. A Negro priest in the south told me that Negro servants spoke of the rejoicing in the homes of racists, and their celebrations of the event. Some places in the South refused to fly flags half-mast. On the other hand I think a lot of decent men in the south have been conscience-stricken and disturbed. Kentucky is not the deep south and hence the reaction here is that of the great part of the nation. But the shock has really been terrible for many many people who were in one way or another weak. Many have had mental breakdowns, probably because of the fact that Kennedy as a symbol had been destroyed and they lost their strength. Or perhaps also from a sense of participation in national guilt.

You may be right about the murder, and it is possible that the investigation may be in many ways frustrated. The Dallas police have obviously been very negligent and stupid, and the stories that have been given out have been widely accepted. But will they hold water?

A curious thing: in the speech which he was going to deliver when he was killed, Kennedy was reporting on the great progress that had been made in every form of armament, and ended by saying that the greatest progress had been made in the measures to stop "guerillas, saboteurs and *assassins*." He was of course speaking of places like Viet Nam. It was strange, after the list of huge intercontinental missiles, hydrogen bombs, polaris submarines and the rest, to reflect that he had been killed by two bullets from a rifle that had cost only a few dollars and had been ordered from a mail order house.

Whatever may be the awful ironies of the case, we have lost in him a reasonable and dependable man, in the power of his mature age, a good and loyal president, courageous and realistic. But above all it is this wiping out of reason by fanaticism that is the disturbing thing. We do not have so much reason in this country that we can afford to lose one of the few that knew how to make use of it consistently in politics.

I am sorry for the grim contents of this letter, and hope that you will not feel too badly on our account. Take care of yourself, and pray for us. I will keep you in my prayers and masses, and especially will include you and all your intentions, with those of the Petits Frères, in my Christmas Masses. Do keep well, do not exhaust yourself. God is near and His truth encompasses us even in the midst of this darkness.

33. TO FR. GODFREY
DIEKMANN, O.S.B.

I want to share what must be your immense satisfaction with the Constitution on Liturgy, pro-
mulgated by Pope Paul at the end of the Council
session recently. In contrast to the Decree on Mass
Media, it is a splendid and lively document, and
of course it represents all that you and *Worship*
have always stood for. So I want to congratulate
you, and to rejoice with you. I am grateful that
God has given you the joy of seeing this. May it
be to all of us a further sign of His marvelous life
and action in His Church, and may it really herald
the true, deep, universal renewal of the spirit of
worship, and the practice of real liturgy at last, on
a wide scale, not just for the few.

A great deal is to be done, for it is only a good
beginning. All is yet to be fashioned. Not being
too much of a pastoral liturgy man, I would not
know what to say about all that, except that the
singing has got to be really alive and I wonder if
the old forms will do? I wonder too if we are yet
ready to create new forms that will be "eternal."
Better perhaps to envisage a long state of transi-
tion and experimentation, and hope that plenty of
freedom will be granted . . . and properly used!

34. TO A PRIEST

You tell me that my article on "The Christian in the Diaspora" strikes you as an expression of defeatism, withdrawal and evasion: you say that in approving of Karl Rahner's ideas I am being too pessimistic and am in fact renouncing the true Christian hope which ought to be mine at this moment when the Council bears witness to new life in the Church and promises great new endeavors and conquests. I certainly do not think that either Rahner or I are defeatists, and I think that one ought to understand the spirit of realistic and sober optimism which informs Rahner's diaspora concept.

The point at issue for Rahner (and for me) is the recognition and acceptance of a new situation, a situation of complete *openness* to the world. It is the situation of the worker-priest or of the Little Brother (of Charles de Foucauld) or, I maintain, of the authentic hermit and also of the kind of monk the first monks were. Simply people like other people, not protected by Roman collars, holy water, surplices, mitres, croziers, and by the conviction that all the world must comply with Canon Law. At the same time this sacrifice of clerical trappings and other ecclesial non-essentials must also be accompanied by a much clearer and more total dedication to Christ on the one hand and a more complete openness to those who are most opposed to us on the other, so that it may mean participation in unpopular causes (for racial justice, civil rights, peace, etc.).

What I am trying to say about the monk is perhaps too paradoxical and too outrageous to be clear, let alone acceptable: but I think the monastic state should be one of complete liberty from the pressures and confusions of "the world" in the bad sense of the word, and even from the more "worldly" side of the Church, so that the monk, isolated and at liberty, can on the one hand give himself to God and to the Word of God, attain to a truly Christian understanding of the needs and sufferings of the men of his time (from his special vantage point of poverty, labor, solitude and insecurity) and also enter into dialogue with those who are not monks and not even Christians.

I suppose that part of the difficulty in communication between us arises from the fact that you are concerned with an apostolate that confronts you at every moment with large groups of people and you are concerned with reaching them all effectively, getting through to them with a message of hope and awakening them to greater love of the Church. I am more concerned with dialogue with selected groups of people—intellectuals, etc. and *not* with large numbers or with a movement. This may sound like an aristocratic approach but I think it is a traditional monastic one. I think the monk is concerned with *personal* contacts with people who exercise influence over groups, rather than directly with groups.

I am definitely not claiming that what we have to do is withdraw into our monasteries and pull the hoods over our heads and say prayers or carry out pleasant liturgical ceremonies for ourselves and a few devotees. On the other hand I do think that if we just try to maintain our situation of privilege and our great monastic and ecclesial front, with big complex organizations and huge expenditures of money to maintain "the image" and to keep going extensive and largely fruitless activities, that we will be doing little for the Church or the world, and we will simply be giving the world something to yawn at, first of all, and later, when they are sufficiently annoyed, to destroy. Now I realize that this last passage may seem offensive and I hasten to assure you that I am not criticizing anyone in particular, least of all any community. What I have said applies to us all to some extent, and of course is also exaggerated and one-sided. It is only a partial example of the mentality I disagree with——the mentality which seeks to carry on according to medieval and theocratic patterns in a world that long since ceased to be medieval and in which the Church is *not* running the show.

Hence I do not think that Christian optimism demands an unlimited confidence in our current projects and movements. However good these may be, they suffer from very serious limitations, and first of all they tend to be associated with the preservation of comforts and privileges in a society that has not exactly distinguished itself for its equity and disinterestedness. Let us face the fact that we priests and monks have been very slow to get involved in the most serious and urgent problems—race, nuclear war, etc., and have looked for easier successes and quicker returns elsewhere— perhaps equating optimism with the hope of quick success.

Christian optimism to my mind is this: full belief and hope in the mercy of God to men in Christ. This mercy is superabundant, and it consists in an overwhelming and total victory over evil, over sin, over death, over the Law as the agent in some sense of sin. Secondly I believe in the God-given power which we have in Christ to share His victory with others, to perform works of faith and love, in the Spirit, to enable our brother to come to the knowledge of Christ, that he may also be liberated from sin, death and judgement to a life of love and praise. This victory reaches mankind of course through the visible Church, but in actual fact there are no limits at all upon the mercy of God and no one can say whether or not some people outside the visible Church are not much more full of the Spirit than many of us others. Consequently it seems to me that the meaning of the diaspora situation consists in recognizing this fact and in realizing how true it is that the Christian and the monk are actually in a position of working out their own salvation and that of the world together with the non-Christian and the non-monk, so that we actually have much to learn from them, and must be open to them, since it is always possible that life-giving grace may come to us through our encounter with them. This is what I mean by the Christian in the diaspora. I am for the diaspora. I prefer it to the closed Medieval hegemony. It may offer much better chances of a real Christian life and brotherhood. Is this pessimism?

On the other hand I definitely eschew what seems to me to be a phony and naive optimism, which consists, grossly speaking, of the following elements: An exaggerated and triumphalist view of the Church in her present, concrete and historical existence: she is regarded as having realized all perfection visibly, as being in her human elements beyond criticism because without spot or wrinkle. She knows all the answers thoroughly, not only the theological answers but the answers to all social, economic, etc., problems. She has nothing to learn from anyone; she is just there to *tell* everyone. She is just about to go into high gear and 1) solve all these problems, 2) embrace all mankind into the visible fold and this is to be done by stepping up our present activities, organizing them better, improving the system, polishing up the apparatus, better magazines, bigger and better schools, more impressive movements, etc. The optimism I distrust is an optimism that sees no further than this and is content to believe that, with these means and a little more energy, the solution to all problems is just around the corner. That we are very soon going to have a big happy well-organized, entirely Christian world. This would be reducing Christian optimism to a rotarian cult of success and visible results, and would leave us with the spurious radiance of clerical Babbits. Note that I am not pinning this oversimplified caricature on Teilhard de Chardin. He is much deeper than this and is not really talking in these terms at all. He is perfectly right in saying that Christian hope is dynamic and is bound to have a deeply transforming effect in the world if it is really put to work there. With this I agree, but it has got to be Christian hope, hope in the Cross and Victory of Christ, not hope in Catholic organizations.

The trouble with getting too involved in movements, organizations and their activity, as I see it, is that one gets immersed in things which are by their very nature deceptive because they tend to promise much more than they can ever achieve, and much more than the Lord wants of them. They become ends in themselves. They become idols, and they tend to extinguish the Spirit. And that goes for the monastic movement itself. Loss of perspective in this can be a grave danger. I think the first thing of all is for monks to be Christians, and I think that perhaps what we need to work on most are the fundamentals, but liberated from the massive accumulation of non-essentials, if not debris.

It all comes down to our actual relationship with our brother. I don't believe in the Abbey of Gethsemani, Inc., but I do believe in my brothers. I stand or fall with them, and I hope to rise with them. I need them and they need me. And all together we need a lot of other people. I need some of the South American poets with whom I correspond, and my friend Lax in Greece, and a Moslem friend, and a lot of others here there and everywhere who have nothing to do with Catholicism. And they need me. And the bonds that unite us are supremely important. It is in this that I am a diaspora Christian and see no way to being anything else. I am all for Teilhard's intuitions in this line. But for the rest I'll go along with Kierkegaard, Guardini, Bonhoeffer, Rahner, etc. Not that this puts me against Teilhard. Please don't involve me in this oversimplification. I am for very much that is in Teilhard but I am not in complete sympathy with the people who are mobilizing a kind of Teilhardian movement. I am certainly not taken in by the naive Teilhardism of Morris West's book *The Shoes of the Fisherman*. I can hardly think of a sillier and more pitiable excuse for optimism than this. It is childish. However I do not want anything I have said in this letter, particularly the deliberately gross caricature of what I do not accept as "optimism," to be interpreted as a closing of doors and refusal to comprehend Teilhard, or an attack on him. Obviously one of the first things that has to be faced is that in a dialogue with Marxism Teilhard is of prime importance (since he is in great part a Marxist himself) but here again there are ambiguities.

Finally as regards the so-called contemplative life, please don't think that I am for a whole lot of introversion and introspection. My novices could tell you enough about that. True, in the past I have been much more inclined to that kind of "contemplation" which looks into the ground of one's being, the Rhenish tradition, John of the Cross etc. My personal vocation tends to be solitary and reflective: but one learns over a period of years to go beyond the limits of a narrow and subjective absorption in one's own "interiority" (ugh). Still, I think there always arises a problem in clash of temperaments on this question and I know a certain type of person is acutely sensitive to any suggestion of anything that seems to point to introversion. In such cases I think it is best to stay off the subject rather than go into a lot of largely futile explanations, which only falsify perspectives still further.

35.   TO A CUBAN POET

Yes, your letter reached me, and I have been thinking about it deeply, as also about your poem about Christ and the Robbers. I have been thinking about these things in silence, at a long distance from the noise of official answers and declamations.

I am alone with the bronze hills and a vast sky, and shadows of pine trees. Sometimes the shadows are alive with golden butterflies. Everywhere is the inscrutable and gentle and very silent face of truth. Nothing is said. In this silence and in this presence I have been reading your poems, and those of F. and E. and O. And I have not been able to find those of R. He should send me more, and all of you please send me new poems. It may take time to get to them in the silence like this, but I will do so. The time is come when the publication of poems is to be like that of pale and very light airborne seeds flowing in the current of forest air through the blue shadows, and falling on the grass where God decrees. I am convinced that we are now already in the time where the printed word is not read, but the paper passed from hand to hand is read eagerly. A time of small letters, hesitant, but serious and personal, and outside of the meaningless dimension of the huge, the monstrous and the cruel.

I like very much F.'s poem on the Transfiguration. It has a great stateliness and seriousness about it. I like also E.'s short poems, especially *la Casa del Pan,* which I intend to translate when I get time (though I am not good at keeping promises like this: I have still not translated any of yours, but I will). And the one about the cockatoos in the shadows: very incisive. F.'s *Anima Viva* is more difficult and I must read it some more. Of O. I like best *Ambas,* so far. I am sorry I cannot find anything of R. here.

I heard from E. and like his elegy for Marilyn Monroe (the sad nonsense and futility of this world here).

Really, the reading of your poems in this silence has been very meaningful and serious: much more serious than the publication of new magazines with poetic manifestoes. I have written something for M.G. on "the poet and freedom," but I wonder sometimes whether such declarations have a

meaning. I am sad at the different kinds of pro-
gramatic affirmations made by poets, and the outcry about freedom from poets who have no concept of what it is all about, who are so absurd as to
think it means freedom to knock themselves out
with dope or something of the sort. Sick. Absurd.
What waste of their opportunities: their freedom
is pure aimlessness and in the end it collapses
in the worst kind of unfreedom and arbitrariness.

I hope you are all well and keep you in my
prayers. May God be with you always, and may
His truth never abandon you, and may your hearts
be fixed in His joy and His light. I will say a Mass
for you all when I can, perhaps on All Saints'
Day. What day is the Feast of La Caridad del
Cobre? I don't think I ever knew.

The Light in which we are one does not change.